Docker High Performance
Second Edition

Complete your Docker journey by optimizing your
application's workflows and performance

Allan Espinosa
Russ McKendrick

BIRMINGHAM - MUMBAI

Docker High Performance
Second Edition

Commissioning Editor: Vijin Boricha
Acquisition Editor: Aditi Gour
Content Development Editor: Roshan Kumar
Technical Editor: Adya Anand
Copy Editor: Safis Editing
Project Coordinator: Namrata Swetta
Proofreader: Safis Editing
Indexer: Tejal Daruwale Soni
Graphics: Jisha Chirayil
Production Coordinator: Jisha Chirayil

First published: January 2016
Second edition: April 2019

Production reference: 1300419

Published by Packt Publishing Ltd.
Livery Place
35 Livery Street
Birmingham
B3 2PB, UK.

ISBN 978-1-78980-721-9

www.packtpub.com

`mapt.io`

Mapt is an online digital library that gives you full access to over 5,000 books and videos, as well as industry leading tools to help you plan your personal development and advance your career. For more information, please visit our website.

Why subscribe?

- Spend less time learning and more time coding with practical eBooks and Videos from over 4,000 industry professionals

- Improve your learning with Skill Plans built especially for you

- Get a free eBook or video every month

- Mapt is fully searchable

- Copy and paste, print, and bookmark content

Packt.com

Did you know that Packt offers eBook versions of every book published, with PDF and ePub files available? You can upgrade to the eBook version at `www.packt.com` and as a print book customer, you are entitled to a discount on the eBook copy. Get in touch with us at `customercare@packtpub.com` for more details.

At `www.packt.com`, you can also read a collection of free technical articles, sign up for a range of free newsletters, and receive exclusive discounts and offers on Packt books and eBooks.

Contributors

About the authors

Allan Espinosa is a DevOps practitioner and an active open source contributor to various distributed system tools, such as Docker and Chef. Allan maintains several Docker images for popular open source software that were popular even before their official release from the upstream open source groups.

Throughout his career, Allan has worked on large distributed systems containing hundreds to thousands of servers in production. He has built scalable applications on various platforms, ranging from large supercomputing centers to production clusters in the enterprise. He is currently managing distributed systems at scale for Bloomberg, where he oversees the company's Hadoop infrastructure. Allan can be contacted through his Twitter handle, `@AllanEspinosa`.

> *I would like to thank my wife, Kana, for the continuous support that allowed me to spend significant time with this project.*

Russ McKendrick is an experienced system administrator who has been working in IT and related industries for over 25 years. During his career, he has had varied responsibilities, from looking after an entire IT infrastructure to providing first-line, second-line, and senior support in both client-facing and internal teams for large organizations.

Russ supports open source systems and tools on public and private clouds at N4Stack, a Node4 company, where he is the practice manager (SRE and DevOps). In his spare time, he has written several books including *Mastering Docker*, *Learn Ansible* and *Kubernetes for Serverless Applications*, all published by Packt Publishing.

About the reviewer

Shashikant Bangera is a lead DevOps architect working for a multinational IT service provider. He specializes in architecting automated, efficient delivery pipelines to help build software rapidly and effectively. He has extensive experience with the cloud, containers, and DevOps tools and process. He has worked across a variety of domains, and designed DevOps processes and automation for large-scale projects. He is an open source enthusiast and has multiple projects under his name on GitHub. He has a master's degree from Welingkar University.

Packt is searching for authors like you

If you're interested in becoming an author for Packt, please visit `authors.packtpub.com` and apply today. We have worked with thousands of developers and tech professionals, just like you, to help them share their insight with the global tech community. You can make a general application, apply for a specific hot topic that we are recruiting an author for, or submit your own idea.

Table of Contents

Preface

Docker is an enterprise-grade container platform that allows you to build and deploy your apps. Its portable format lets you run your code anywhere, from your desktop workstation, to popular cloud computing providers. This book will help you realize the full potential of Docker.

In this book, you will learn a lot about how Docker works. You will learn the basics of Docker, along with some of the fundamental concepts of web operations. You will gain knowledge of Docker and the relevant operating system concepts to get a deeper understanding of what is happening behind the scenes. You will also learn a lot about the tools to deploy and troubleshoot our Docker containers in production in a scalable and manageable fashion.

Who this book is for

If you are a software developer with a good understanding of managing Docker services and the Linux file system, and are looking for ways to optimize working with Docker containers, then this is the book for you. Developers fascinated by containers and workflow automation will also benefit from this book.

What this book covers

Chapter 1, *Preparing Docker Hosts*, helps you familiarize yourself with Docker Engine and how to prepare a Docker host. We will then build a PKI to ensure secure communication between our Docker host and our Docker client workstation. We will also build a small Docker Swarm cluster, consisting of multiple Docker hosts.

Chapter 2, *Configuring Docker with Chef*, shows how to automate the configuration of our Docker deployments. We will also use Chef, a piece of configuration management software, to manage Docker hosts in scale.

Chapter 3, *Monitoring Docker*, helps us to understand the importance of monitoring and collecting metrics in Prometheus. We will also learn how to consolidate logs in an ELK stack.

Chapter 4, *Optimizing Docker Images*, discusses optimizing our Docker images and improving our development workflow. We will also learn to reduce image deployment time and improve image build time.

Chapter 5, *Deploying Containers*, looks at how we can use Jenkins to build, distribute, and deploy our containerized application. We will also learn to build and deploy a simple application using a three-stage pipeline.

Chapter 6, *Benchmarking*, helps us create benchmarks to gauge the performance of our Docker application.

Chapter 7, *Load Balancing*, talks about how to scale out our Docker applications to increase our capacity. We will use load balancers, which are a key component in the architecture of various web scale applications. We will also learn to balance load with NGINX.

Chapter 8, *Troubleshooting Containers*, inspects containers with Docker exec, and help us understand what debugging is, along with other container debugging tools.

Chapter 9, *Onto Production*, wraps up the book by teaching us how to perform web operations. We will also learn to deploy and scale our applications.

To get the most out of this book

1. A Linux workstation with a recent kernel is needed to serve as a host for Docker CE 18.09.0. This book uses CentOS 7 as its base operating system to install and set up Docker.
2. More details on how to get Docker up and running is covered in Chapter 1, Preparing Docker Hosts.

Download the example code files

You can download the example code files for this book from your account at www.packt.com. If you purchased this book elsewhere, you can visit www.packt.com/support and register to have the files emailed directly to you.

You can download the code files by following these steps:

1. Log in or register at `www.packt.com`.
2. Select the **SUPPORT** tab.
3. Click on **Code Downloads & Errata**.
4. Enter the name of the book in the **Search** box and follow the onscreen instructions.

Once the file is downloaded, please make sure that you unzip or extract the folder using the latest version of:

- WinRAR/7-Zip for Windows
- Zipeg/iZip/UnRarX for Mac
- 7-Zip/PeaZip for Linux

The code bundle for the book is also hosted on GitHub at `https://github.com/PacktPublishing/Docker-High-Performance-Second-Edition`. In case there's an update to the code, it will be updated on the existing GitHub repository.

We also have other code bundles from our rich catalog of books and videos available at `https://github.com/PacktPublishing/`. Check them out!

Download the color images

We also provide a PDF file that has color images of the screenshots/diagrams used in this book. You can download it here: `https://www.packtpub.com/sites/default/files/downloads/9781789807219_ColorImages.pdf`.

Conventions used

There are a number of text conventions used throughout this book.

`CodeInText`: Indicates code words in text, database table names, folder names, filenames, file extensions, pathnames, dummy URLs, user input, and Twitter handles. Here is an example: "First, we will create a directory for our PKI and generate the CA's private key in a file called `ca-key.pem`."

A block of code is set as follows:

```
{
    "tlsverify": true,
    "tlscacert": "/etc/docker/ca.pem",
    "tlskey": "/etc/docker/server-key.pem",
    "tlscert": "/etc/docker/server.pem"
}
```

Any command-line input or output is written as follows:

```
dockerhost$ systemctl daemon-reload
dockerhost$ systemctl restart docker.service
```

Bold: Indicates a new term, an important word, or words that you see onscreen. For example, words in menus or dialog boxes appear in the text like this. Here is an example: " In the form field labeled **Name**, set the value to **Unicorn Capacity**."

Warnings or important notes appear like this.

Tips and tricks appear like this.

Get in touch

Feedback from our readers is always welcome.

General feedback: If you have questions about any aspect of this book, mention the book title in the subject of your message and email us at customercare@packtpub.com.

Errata: Although we have taken every care to ensure the accuracy of our content, mistakes do happen. If you have found a mistake in this book, we would be grateful if you would report this to us. Please visit www.packt.com/submit-errata, selecting your book, clicking on the Errata Submission Form link, and entering the details.

Piracy: If you come across any illegal copies of our works in any form on the Internet, we would be grateful if you would provide us with the location address or website name. Please contact us at copyright@packt.com with a link to the material.

If you are interested in becoming an author: If there is a topic that you have expertise in and you are interested in either writing or contributing to a book, please visit authors.packtpub.com.

Reviews

Please leave a review. Once you have read and used this book, why not leave a review on the site that you purchased it from? Potential readers can then see and use your unbiased opinion to make purchase decisions, we at Packt can understand what you think about our products, and our authors can see your feedback on their book. Thank you!

For more information about Packt, please visit packt.com.

Preparing Docker Hosts

Docker allows us to deliver applications to our customers faster. It simplifies the workflows needed to get code from development to production by being able to easily create and launch Docker containers. This chapter will be a quick refresher on how to get our environment ready to run Docker-based development and operations workflow by doing the following:

- Preparing a Docker host
- Enabling remote access to Docker hosts
- Building a Docker Swarm cluster

Most of the parts of this chapter are concepts that we are already familiar with and these are readily available in the Docker documentation website. This chapter shows selected commands and interactions with the Docker host that will be used in the succeeding chapters.

Preparing a Docker host

It is assumed that we are already familiar on how to set up a Docker host. For most of the chapters of this book, we will run against the following environment unless mentioned explicitly:

- Operating System: CentOS 7.5
- Docker version: 18.09.0

The following commands display the operating system and Docker Engine version running inside our Docker host:

```
$ ssh dockerhost
dockerhost$ lsb_release -a
LSB Version:  :core-4.1-amd64:core-4.1-noarch
Distributor ID:    CentOS
Description: CentOS Linux release 7.5.1804 (Core)
Release:     7.5.1804
Codename:    Core
dockerhost$ docker version
 Version:           18.09.0
 API version:       1.39
 Go version:        go1.10.4
 Git commit:        4d60db4
 Built:             Wed Nov  7 00:48:22 2018
 OS/Arch:           linux/amd64
 Experimental:      false

Server: Docker Engine - Community
 Engine:
  Version:          18.09.0
  API version:      1.39 (minimum version 1.12)
  Go version:       go1.10.4
  Git commit:       4d60db4
  Built:            Wed Nov  7 00:19:08 2018
  OS/Arch:          linux/amd64
  Experimental:     false
```

 If we haven't set up our Docker environment, we can follow the instructions in the Docker website found in `https://docs.docker.com/install/linux/docker-ce/centos/` to prepare our Docker host.

Enabling remote access

Instead of logging in remotely to our Docker host to run containers, we will access the Docker host by enabling the remote API in Docker Engine. This allows us to manage our Docker containers from our client workstation or continuous delivery server. We will then interact with our Docker host to represent our production environment. The remote API will then be used from our client workstation to perform deployments of our Docker containers.

This section will cover the steps to secure and enable remote access to our Docker host:

- Setting up a certificate authority
- Reconfiguring Docker Engine to enable remote access
- Configuring the Docker client for remote access

Setting up a certificate authority

For the rest of this section, we will be installing TLS certificates in both our Docker host server and client. To ensure trusted communication between the server and client, we will be setting up a **Public Key Infrastructure** (**PKI**). This will allow both the Docker engine running in our host and our Docker client to make the connection to verify the identity of each other.

The first step in building the PKI is setting up the **Certificate Authority** (**CA**). A CA is a trusted third party that issues digital certificates to members of our PKI, namely our Docker host and client.

In the next few steps, we will set up our CA inside of our client workstation:

1. First, we will create a directory for our PKI and generate the CA's private key in a file called `ca-key.pem`:

```
client$ mkdir ~/ca
client$ cd ~/ca
client$ openssl genrsa -aes256 -out ca-key.pem 4096

Generating RSA private key, 4096 bit long modulus
.....................................++
.................................................++
e is 65537 (0x10001)
Enter pass phrase for ca-key.pem: ****
Verifying - Enter pass phrase for ca-key.pem: ****
```

We need to remember the passphrases set for our CA's private key, as we will always need them for the rest of this chapter.

2. Next, we make sure that this private key is secure by restricting read and write access to us:

```
client$ chmod 600 ca-key.pem
client$ ls -l ca-key.pem
-rw-------. 1 dockeruser group 3326 Dec  2 20:45 ca-key.pem
```

3. Finally, we will generate a certificate for our CA that is self-signed. Let's type the following command to place the self-signed certificate in a file called `ca.pem`:

```
client$ openssl req -key ca-key.pem -new -x509  \
-subj '/CN=Certificate Authority' \
-sha256 -days 365 -out ca.pem
Enter pass phrase for ca-key.pem: ****
```

We now have a CA, and we will be distributing its `ca.pem` certificate to our Docker host and client later in this section. For now, let's inspect the generate certificate:

```
client$ cat ca.pem
```

```
-----BEGIN CERTIFICATE-----
MIIFEzCCAvugAwIBAgIJAM19ce5sap+kMA0GCSqGSIb3DQEBCwUAMCAxHjAcBgNV
BAMMFUN1cnRpZm1jYXR1IEF1dGhvcm10eTAeFw0xODEyMDYwMzQ5MTNaFw0xOTEy
MDYwMzQ5MTNaMCAxHjAcBgNVBAMMFUN1cnRpZm1jYXR1IEF1dGhvcm10eTCCAiIw
DQYJKoZIhvcNAQEBBQADggIPADCCAgoCggIBAKCESs7QpRZ78v8p2nKomCGABqCN
b3E0vBpjveTnjA4kOEWVsHloq2o66yuuNff75GNWghzq791KyKJOy/dehNL9DauA
DD3DJh0+uaOGn547W827Z37wJ64acNyvIQjyiyeLrpF4BzzxaZ/AJFVgqar5Kuqc
qiOG3GUYcnfu6mpmlKoa1XqBtSQ+A2fd4/mpXC0zrDrz9MSEOCs5/Xm6/faexYae
V8gBkCYWiUVUi+RRRc2vU1Lzui15FsXmD3kNHCjNIbYIoyqKMzbTJjEffhN+5B/V
Rc3qfRmfoEv8P0Hc4Wx55qH8BLWwhvNFAZ+nre+j7zPz+dTfLVyveOPxErHaI1V8
WH9qEVf+haNqUBrjNCuL+xyVNx7evPygD88jyZDWLK5Y0JTh2GSPqMeVi3hSKzNP
GbVjT8tmkCUEsYbSJg2vkPYJR4aC8LLdJsjr7wkWBF1IcYYZpLo3EsUnkjNi7MGS
pGdLob3UToekXaA1D6esDh1EB+3Tt/RWJkS91ijUiDs2kTSmDfnxUQGyeD4wx/rj
1PFRSLdUUYiFcdI5VegZVSqYxW/Qw2/t+GvoLkrOrggqY1f++XUgK5hSoT8EqgiG
SjapkgphMEquVP8U1Z3jC0VmgwFnRUEdqau6yLWMYG6TvLkyVi1Vmfam7CoB1aDn
TccUszk+rezX+1nJAgMBAAGjUDBOMB0GA1UdDgQWBBTrqfPKO0i2peZ6Hd/BYOMq
WXD9kDAfBgNVHSMEGDAWgBTrqfPKO0i2peZ6Hd/BYOMqWXD9kDAMBgNVHRMEBTAD
AQH/MA0GCSqGSIb3DQEBCwUAA4ICAQCa6SPGncEZSWu0WLfkh1mERa9JfBQzJFpv
1E7M3tZeFyJS7LfXdcf9WEAaWqTpha87A+5g9uBi/whYk47dyTik07/k+CyF112i
9GXK8j/UNCjAMOS1uOCxpIsmMXp2Dn+ma21msN1K/1HK0ZhGWB9ZDggvdzRRPjic
Dq3aQ49ATHQHGg9cqgZO0zXtcQYaHfCNds5YLNVL66eDhuN91V2MEqWtRDHfr0vA
F3K1dXfQ/clnrjGLqo7a3oR1R4QofQ03bV+PRIgub+13Fee1D68BqF9dLRjUABd2
zm5OzNAmmHPSGWGvOxylvPrUS0u1UzMUWdoXN85SDdLHFXTXwpbD/GgqK+Y3BTgO
7d+mOoTHVEdw2gUXLaqeEchBge2Kh/LQtiN7Zp8OY7snX66Z8tF6W2MKhnSpDzcW
J4WMbmaRqsTEeaRk0aTWkhBZukSZf4zjaa/abF+iRvU5c10GS9GmYfuGqg3Tlj+Xo
JZNuKp9HzOPaj8qiD0DJW9EnuZ24zzpDSiSdmOdARcaaFFKhW8i+SVP6VqrAR3Nb
OL8ne6w6kdoiq4+hPKfWVS9Yh0aQstJMNP91Nnw3J+aRz9eN03jp1/z18vHhW/x1
nYJrB2K1C7SOnUT7TMJr4O5Aw1SidxMH6NLiiC1jbTWXDMuYL8UghDIk9Ne/WhBd
qg0sW+boLw==
-----END CERTIFICATE-----
```

Enabling remote access in Docker Engine

Now that we have a CA for our PKI, we can use this CA to verify the identity of our Docker host. The following steps will prepare the identity of our Docker host:

1. First, we log in to our Docker host. In here, we will generate a private key that will secure the remote API being served by running Docker Engine. The following command will save the private key into a file called `/etc/docker/server-key.pem`:

   ```
   dockerhost$ openssl genrsa -out /etc/docker/server-key.pem 2048

   Generating RSA private key, 2048 bit long modulus
   ...............................+++
   ........+++
   e is 65537 (0x10001)
   ```

2. Next, we make sure that this file is secure and can only be accessed by the Docker Engine daemon (through the root user):

   ```
   dockerhost$ chmod 600 /etc/docker/server-key.pem
   dockerhost$ ls -l /etc/docker/server-key.pem

   -rw-------. 1 root root 1675 Dec  2 21:09 /etc/docker/server-key.pem
   ```

3. Now that the private key is ready, we will use this file to generate a **Certificate Signing Request (CSR)**. `openssl req` following command will generate a CSR:

   ```
   dockerhost$ openssl req -key /etc/docker/server-key.pem
   -new -subj "/CN=dockerhost" -sha256 -out
   dockerhost.csr
   dockerhost$ ls -l dockerhost.csr
   -rw-r--r--. 1 root root 891 Dec  2 21:33 dockerhost.csr
   ```

4. Next, we go back to our client workstation where our CA's files are hosted. In here, we will download the CSR from our Docker host:

   ```
   client$ scp dockerhost:~/dockerhost.csr dockerhost.csr
   dockerhost.csr               100%  891     1.5MB/s   00:00
   ```

5. We now prepare an OpenSSL configuration `server-ext.cnf` file that indicates that the certificates our CA will issue are used for server authentication:

   ```
   extendedKeyUsage = serverAuth
   ```

6. Finally, we can sign the CSR with our CA. The following command will place our Docker host's signed certificate in a file called `dockerhost.pem`:

```
client$ cd ~/ca
client$ openssl x509 -req -CA ca.pem -CAkey ca-key.pem \
-CAcreateserial -extfile server-ext.cnf \
-in dockerhost.csr -out dockerhost.pem
Signature ok
subject=/CN=dockerhost
Getting CA Private Key
Enter pass phrase for ca-key.pem: ****
```

Now that we have the identity of our Docker host verified by our CA, we can now enable the secure TCP port in our Docker host. We will bring up the secure remote API with the following steps:

1. Let's now go back into our Docker host. Here, we will copy the certificates of our Docker host and CA from our client workstation:

```
dockerhost$ scp client:~/ca/ca.pem /etc/docker/ca.pem
ca.pem                        100% 1911      1.1MB/s   00:00
dockerhost$ scp client:~/ca/dockerhost.pem /etc/docker/server.pem
dockerhost.pem                          100% 1428      1.2MB/s   00:00
```

2. Now that our TLS assets are in place, let's now reconfigure the Docker Engine daemon file, `/etc/docker/daemon.json`, to use those certificates:

```
{
  "tlsverify": true,
  "tlscacert": "/etc/docker/ca.pem",
  "tlskey": "/etc/docker/server-key.pem",
  "tlscert": "/etc/docker/server.pem"
}
```

3. Next, we configure the Docker Engine daemon to listen to a secure port by creating a `systemd` override file `/etc/systemd/system/docker.service.d/override.conf`:

```
[Service]
ExecStart=
ExecStart=/usr/bin/dockerd -H unix:// -H tcp://0.0.0.0:2376
```

4. Finally, we are now ready to restart Docker Engine:

```
dockerhost$ systemctl daemon-reload
dockerhost$ systemctl restart docker.service
```

Our Docker host is now ready and serving a secure API.

Connecting remotely from the Docker client

Now that our Docker host is secure, it won't respond to requests from our Docker client yet. The Docker host will only respond to requests being made by clients verified by our CA.

The following steps will generate an identity for our Docker client:

1. First, let's generate the private key of our Docker client in `~/.docker/key.pem`:

   ```
   client$ openssl genrsa -out ~/.docker/key.pem 4096

   Generating RSA private key, 4096 bit long modulus
   ..................++
          ..........................................................++
   e is 65537 (0x10001)
   ```

2. Next, we make sure that this private key is restricted to us for viewing:

   ```
   client$ chmod 600 ~/.docker/key.pem
   ```

3. We now generate the CSR for client in a file called `client.csr`:

   ```
   client$ openssl req -subj '/CN=client' -new \
   -key ~/.docker/key.pem -out client.csr
   ```

4. Now that our CSR is ready, we will now create an OpenSSL configuration to indicate that certificates will be used for client authentication. The OpenSSL command following creates this configuration in a file called `~/ca/client-ext.cnf`:

   ```
   extendedKeyUsage = clientAuth
   ```

5. Finally, we are ready to issue the certificate for our Docker client. The following command writes our Docker client's certificate to `~/.docker/cert.pem`:

   ```
   client$ openssl x509 -req -CA ca.pem
       -CAkey ca-key.pem -CAcreateserial
       -extfile client-ext.cnf -in
       ~/client.csr -out ~/.docker/cert.pem
       Signature ok
       subject=/CN=client
       Getting CA Private Key
       Enter pass phrase for ca-key.pem: ****
   ```

6. To complete our client's TLS configuration, we will also deploy our CA's certificate in our ~/.docker directory file:

```
client$ cp ca.pem ~/.docker/ca.pem
```

7. Finally, we indicate to our Docker client that we will be connecting securely to our remote Docker host by exporting the following environment variables:

```
client$ export DOCKER_HOST=tcp://dockerhost:2376
client$ export DOCKER_TLS_VERIFY=true
```

Congratulations! We now have a secure communication channel between our Docker client and Docker host. To verify the connection, we can run the following command and show information about our remote Docker host:

```
client$ docker info
```

Building a Docker Swarm cluster

Docker introduced swarm mode to its Docker engine from version 1.12.0. Docker Swarm allows us to pool together multiple Docker hosts to deploy our containers in a scalable and high availability way. In this section, we will build a small Docker Swarm cluster.

Let's dive into building our cluster with the following steps:

1. First, we will go to our Docker host and initialize it as a manager. manager is responsible for maintaining the state of our Docker Swarm cluster. It also dispatches tasks to other Docker hosts in our cluster. Let's type the following command to begin the initialization:

```
dockerhost$ docker swarm init
Swarm initialized: current node (w49smc2ciy100gaecgx77yir3)
is now a manager

To add a worker to this swarm, run the following command:

docker swarm join --token SWMTKN-1-4wbs...aq2r \
172.16.132.187:2377
```

The preceding command generated a token that will be used by other Docker hosts to join our cluster.

2. Next, we will go to a new Docker host called `node1`. We use the token from the previous step to make this Docker host join our Docker Swarm cluster as a `worker`. Workers are members of the cluster that are responsible for running our containers. Let's now type the following command to make this new node join our cluster:

```
node1$ docker swarm join --token SWMTKN-1-4...aq2r \
172.16.132.187:2377
This node joined a swarm as a worker.
```

 We can scale out our Docker Swarm cluster by adding more managers and workers using the same Docker Swarm `join` command. More details can be found in the upstream Docker documentation at `https://docs.docker.com/engine/swarm/join-nodes`.

We have now finished setting up our Docker Swarm cluster. Let's go back to our Docker client workstation and confirm the members of our cluster:

```
client$ docker node ls
ID         HOSTNAME     STATUS  AVAILABILITY MANAGER STATUS ENGINE VERSION
w49smc * dockerhost Ready    Active       Leader         18.09.0
2e0aif   node1        Ready    Active                      18.09.0
```

Summary

Hopefully, at this point, we have become familiar with interacting with Docker Engine. We have prepared a Docker host where we will run our containers. We built a PKI to ensure secure communication between our Docker host and our Docker client workstation, and we built a small Docker Swarm cluster consisting of multiple Docker hosts.

We accomplished all of this by logging in to servers and manually typing configuration commands. In the next chapter, we'll learn to automate provisioning these Docker hosts—and save us from typing!

Configuring Docker with Chef

By now, we are already familiar with the various aspects of the Docker ecosystem. The Docker host has several configuration parameters. However, manually configuring Docker hosts is a slow and error-prone process. We will have problems scaling our Docker deployments in production if we don't have an automation strategy in place.

In this chapter, we will learn the concept of configuration management to solve this problem. We will use Chef, a configuration management software, to manage Docker hosts in scale. This chapter will cover the following topics:

- Importance of configuration management
- Using Chef
- Provisioning Docker hosts
- Configuring Docker Swarm mode
- Alternative automation tools

Importance of configuration management

The Docker Engine has several parameters to tune, such as cgroups, memory, CPU, filesystems, networking, and so on. Identifying which Docker containers run on which Docker hosts is another aspect of configuration. Getting the combination of parameters to optimize our application will take time.

Replicating all the preceding configuration items to another Docker host is difficult to perform manually. We might not remember all the steps required to create a host, and it is an error-prone and slow process. Creating documentation to capture this process doesn't help either because such artifacts tend to get stale over time.

If we cannot provision new Docker hosts in a timely and reliable manner, we will have no space to scale out our Docker application. Therefore, it's important to prepare and configure our Docker hosts in a consistent and fast manner. Otherwise, Docker's ability to create container packages for our application will become useless quite quickly.

Configuration management is a strategy to manage the changes happening in all aspects of our application, and it reports and audits the changes made to our system. This does not only apply when developing our application. For our case, it records all the changes to our Docker hosts. Docker, in a sense, accomplishes the following aspects of configuration management for our application:

- Docker containers reproduce any environment for our application, from development to staging, testing, and production.
- Building Docker images is a simple way to make application changes and have them deployed to all environments.
- Docker enables all team members to get information about our application and make the needed changes to deliver the software efficiently to customers. By inspecting the `Dockerfile`, they can know which part of the application needs to be updated and what it needs in order to run properly.
- Docker tracks any change in our environment to a particular Docker image. Then, it traces it back to the corresponding version of the `Dockerfile`. It traces what the change is, who made it, and when it was made.

However, what about the Docker host running our application? Just as a `Dockerfile` allows us to manage our application's environment in version control, configuration management tools can describe our Docker hosts in code. It simplifies the process to create Docker hosts. In the case of scaling out our Docker application, we can recreate a new Docker host from scratch easily. When there is a hardware failure, we can bring up new Docker hosts somewhere else from their known configuration. Configuration management enables us to manage our Docker deployments in scale.

In the next section, we will be setting up Chef as the configuration management system for our Docker infrastructure.

Using Chef

Chef is a configuration management tool that provides a domain-specific language to model the configuration of our infrastructure. Each configuration item in our infrastructure is modeled as a resource. A resource is basically a Ruby method that accepts several parameters in a block. The following example resource describes installing the `docker-engine` package:

```
package 'docker-engine' do
  action :install
end
```

These resources are then written together in Ruby source files called *recipes*. When running a recipe against a server (a Docker host in our case), all the defined resources are executed to reach its desired state configuration.

Some Chef recipes may depend on other supplemental items, such as configuration templates and other recipes. All this information is gathered in cookbooks together with the recipes. A cookbook is a fundamental unit of distributing configuration and policy to our servers.

We will write Chef recipes to represent the desired state configuration of our Docker hosts. Our recipes will be organized in Chef cookbooks to distribute them to our infrastructure. However, first, let's prepare our Chef environment so that we can start describing our Docker-based infrastructure in recipes. A Chef environment consists of three things:

- A Chef server
- A workstation
- A node

The next few subsections will give you a detailed description of each component. Then, we will set them up to prepare our Chef environment to be able to manage our Docker host.

 There are more details of setting up a Chef environment that are outside this chapter's scope. More information can be found at the Chef documentation website at `http://docs.chef.io`.

Signing up for a Chef server

The Chef server is the central repository of cookbooks and other policy items governing our entire infrastructure. It contains metadata about the infrastructure that we are managing. In our case, the Chef server contains the cookbook, policy, and metadata on our Docker host.

To prepare a Chef server, we will simply sign up for a hosted Chef server. A free Chef server account allows us to manage up to five nodes in our infrastructure. Follow the next few steps to prepare a hosted Chef server account:

1. Go to `https://manage.chef.io/signup` and fill out the form for our account details as shown in the following screenshot:

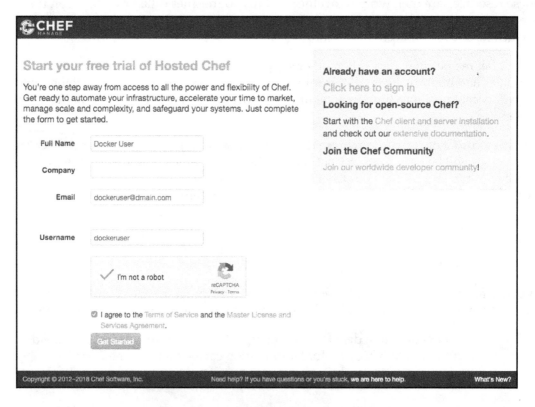

2. After creating a user account, the hosted Chef server will now prompt us to create an organization. Organizations are simply used to manage role-based access control for our Chef server. Create an organization by providing the details on the form and click on the **Create Organization** button.

3. We are now almost done getting our hosted Chef server account. Finally, click on
   Download Starter Kit. This will download a ZIP file containing our starter
   `chef-repo`. We will talk more about the `chef-repo` in the next section:

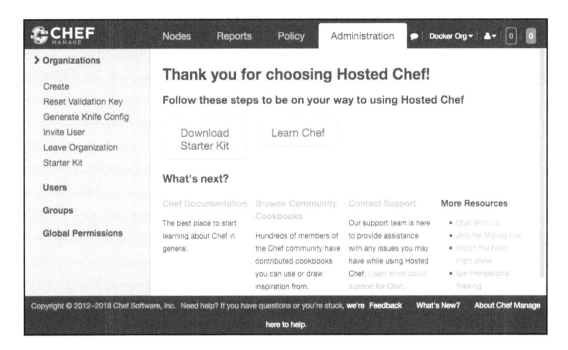

Setting up our workstation

The second part of our Chef environment is the *workstation*. The workstation is used to interact with the Chef server. This is where we will do most of the preparation work and create the code to send to the Chef server. In our workstation, we will prepare the configuration items of our infrastructure in a Chef repository.

The Chef repository contains all the information needed to interact and synchronize with the Chef server. It contains the private key and other configuration files needed to authenticate and interact with the Chef server. These files will be found in the `.chef` directory of our Chef repository. It also contains the cookbooks that we will write and synchronize later with the Chef server in the `cookbooks/` directory. There are other files and directories inside a Chef repository, such as data bags, roles, and environments as well. However, it is enough, for now, to know about the cookbooks and authentication files to be able to configure our Docker host.

Do you remember the starter kit we downloaded in the previous section? You need to unzip this file to extract our chef-repo. We should have the following files described in the directory tree:

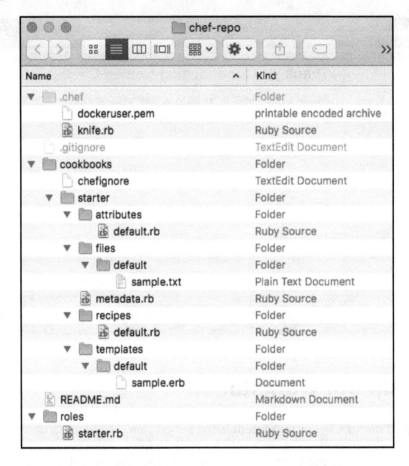

Another important component in our workstation is the **Chef Development Kit**. It contains all the programs needed to read all the configuration in our chef-repo and interact with the Chef server. Convenient programs to create, develop, and test our cookbooks are also available in the **Chef Development Kit**. We will use various programs in the development kit throughout the rest of this chapter.

Now, let's download the **Chef Development Kit** from https://downloads.chef.io/chefdk according to our workstation's platform.

Next, open the downloaded installer. Install the **Chef Development Kit** according to the prompts from our platform. Finally, confirm that the installation was successful with the following command:

```
$ chef -v
Chef Development Kit Version: 3.5.13
chef-client version: 14.7.17
delivery version: master (6862f27aba89109a9630f0b6c6798efec56b4efe)
berks version: 7.0.6
kitchen version: 1.23.2
inspec version: 3.0.52
```

Now that we have set up our workstation, let's go to our `chef-repo/` directory to prepare the last component of our Chef environment.

Bootstrap nodes

The last part of our Chef environment is the nodes. A node is any computer that is managed by Chef. It can be a physical machine, a virtual machine, a server in the cloud, or a networking device. In our case, our Docker host is a node. In the next few steps, we will configure the following Docker hosts:

- `dockerhost`: Will serve as our Docker Swarm Manager
- `node1`: Will connect as a Docker Swarm Node to our cluster

The central component for any node to be managed by Chef is the `chef-client`. It connects to the Chef server to download the necessary files to bring our node to its configuration state. When a `chef-client` is run on our node, it performs the following steps:

1. It registers and authenticates the node with the Chef server
2. It gathers system information in our node to create a node object
3. Then, it synchronizes the Chef cookbooks needed by our node
4. It compiles the resources by loading our node's needed recipes
5. Next, it executes all the resources and performs the corresponding actions to configure our node
6. Finally, it reports the result of the `chef-client` run back to the Chef server and other configured notification endpoints

Now, let's prepare our Docker host as a node by bootstrapping it from our workstation. The bootstrapping process will log in to our node and install the `chef-client`. Run the following command to get this bootstrap process started:

```
$ cd ~/chef-repo
$ knife bootstrap dockerhost -N dockerhost
Creating new client for dockerhost
Creating new node for dockerhost
Connecting to dockerhost
dockerhost -----> Installing Chef Omnibus (-v 14)
...
dockerhost Installing chef 14
dockerhost installing with rpm...
dockerhost warning: /tmp/install.sh.24627/chef-14.7.17-1.el7.x86_64.rpm:
Header V4 DSA/SHA1 Signature, key ID 83ef826a: NOKEY
dockerhost Preparing...
############################### [100%]
dockerhost Updating / installing...
dockerhost    1:chef-14.7.17-1.el7
############################### [100%]
dockerhost Thank you for installing Chef!
dockerhost Starting the first Chef Client run...
dockerhost Starting Chef Client, version 14.7.17
dockerhost resolving cookbooks for run list: []
dockerhost Synchronizing Cookbooks:
dockerhost Installing Cookbook Gems:
dockerhost Compiling Cookbooks...
dockerhost [2018-12-09T03:18:19+00:00] WARN: Node dockerhost has an empty
run list.
dockerhost Converging 0 resources
dockerhost
dockerhost Running handlers:
dockerhost Running handlers complete
dockerhost Chef Client finished, 0/0 resources updated in 03 seconds
```

As we can note in the preceding command, the bootstrapping process did two things. First, it installed and configured the `chef-client` on our Docker host node. Next, it started the `chef-client` to synchronize its desired state with our Chef server. As we haven't assigned any designed state yet to our Docker host, it didn't do anything.

Finally, let us provision the rest of our Docker hosts:

```
$ knife bootstrap node1 -N node1
```

We can customize this bootstrap process according to our needs. More information on how to use `knife bootstrap` can be found at `http://docs.chef.io/knife_bootstrap.html`. In some cases, cloud providers have a deep Chef integration already out of the box. So, instead of `knife bootstrap`, we will just use the cloud provider's SDK. There, we just need to specify that we want to have Chef integrated. We will provide it with the information, such as the chef-client's `client.rb` configuration and validation keys' credentials.

Our Docker host is now properly registered to the Chef server, ready to grab its configuration. Go to `https://manage.chef.io/organizations/dockerorg/nodes/dockerhost` to check our Docker host as a node in our Chef environment, as shown in the following screenshot:

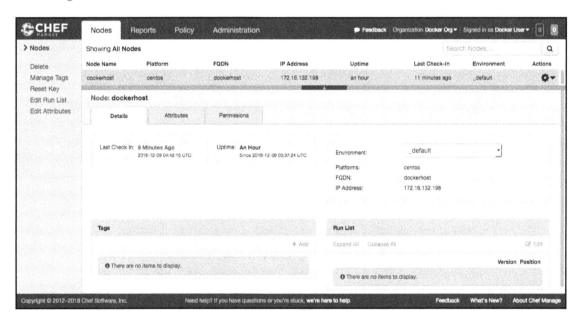

In the next section, we will be specifying the configuration of our Docker hosts with Chef.

Configuring the Docker host

Now that we have all the components of our Chef environment set up properly, we can start writing Chef recipes to actually describe what configuration our Docker hosts should have. In addition, we will leapfrog our productivity by taking advantage of existing Chef cookbooks in the Chef ecosystem. As Docker is a popular infrastructure stack to deploy, we can use cookbooks in the wild that allow us to configure our Docker hosts. Chef cookbooks provided by the community can be found in the Chef Supermarket. We can go to `http://supermarket.chef.io` to discover other cookbooks that we can readily use.

In this section, we will learn how to write Chef recipes and apply them to our node.

Writing Chef recipes

The next few steps show us how to write the Chef recipe for our Docker host:

1. Let us use the Chef development kit's `chef generate cookbook` command to generate a boilerplate for our cookbook. After entering the `cookbooks` directory, issue the following command:

```
$ cd cookbooks
$ chef generate cookbook dockerhost
Generating cookbook dockerhost
- Ensuring correct cookbook file content
- Ensuring delivery configuration
- Ensuring correct delivery build cookbook content

Your cookbook is ready. Type `cd dockerhost` to enter it.

There are several commands you can run to get started locally
developing and testing your cookbook.
Type `delivery local --help` to see a full list.

Why not start by writing a test? Tests for the default recipe are
stored at:

test/integration/default/default_test.rb

If you'd prefer to dive right in, the default recipe can be found
at:

recipes/default.rb
```

The boilerplate cookbook directory structure will look similar to the following screenshot:

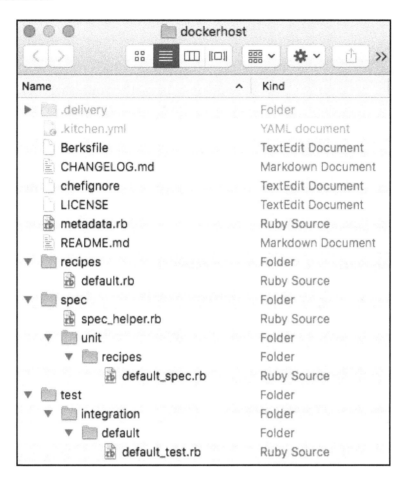

2. Next, we will prepare to edit our cookbook. Change our working directory to the cookbook we created earlier using the following command:

   ```
   $ cd dockerhost
   ```

3. Install the `docker` cookbook from the Chef supermarket as our dependency. This cookbook provides additional resource definitions that can be used in our recipes. We will use them later as building blocks to set up our Docker host. To add the dependencies, update the `metadata.rb` file, as follows:

   ```
   name 'dockerhost'
   maintainer 'The Authors'
   ```

```
maintainer_email 'you@example.com'
license 'all_rights'
description 'Installs/Configures a dockerhost'
long_description 'Installs/Configures a dockerhost'
version '0.1.0'

depends 'docker', '~> 4.8'
```

The `metadata.rb` file provides metadata about our Chef cookbooks. The information in the metadata provides hints to the Chef server so that the cookbook can be properly deployed to our nodes. For more information on how to configure metadata to our Chef cookbooks, visit `http://docs.chef.io/config_rb_metadata.html`.

4. We will now create a Chef recipe in `recipes/base.rb` to describe the basic configuration of our Docker hosts. The content of the following recipe will install and start the Docker Engine from the Docker CE's YUM repository:

```
yum_repository 'docker-stable' do
  description 'Docker CE Stable'
  baseurl 'https://download.docker.com/linux'\
          '/centos/7/$basearch/stable'
  gpgkey 'https://download.docker.com/linux/centos/gpg'
end

docker_service 'default' do
  version '18.09.0'
  install_method 'package'
  setup_docker_repo false
  action %w(create start)
end
```

5. Now that our cookbook is ready, we will create a Chef Policyfile to manage the packaging of our cookbook and its dependencies. We will create a policy called `policies/base.rb` to describe the base setup of our Docker host:

```
name 'base'

default_source :supermarket
cookbook 'dockerhost', path: '../cookbooks/dockerhost'

run_list 'dockerhost::base'
```

6. Now that we have our dependencies declared, we can download them by issuing the following command:

```
$ cd ~/chef-repo
$ chef install policies/base.rb
Building policy base
Expanded run list: recipe[dockerhost::base]
Caching Cookbooks...
Installing dockerhost >= 0.0.0 from path
Using       docker      4.8.0

Lockfile written to ./policies/base.lock.json
Policy revision id: 67435037674caf004468b9a775eb44
```

We are now done creating our base policy to describe our Docker host. Our last step generated a Chef Policyfile lock `policies/base.lock.json` that represents the bundle of cookbooks that we used for this policy.

Push Chef policies

The final stage is to apply this policy to our Docker hosts in order to pick up the desired configuration. We will perform the following steps to achieve this:

1. First, we upload the policy to our Chef server in a policy group called `production`. Note that in the output of the following command, the `docker` cookbook that we depend on will also be automatically uploaded:

```
$ chef push production policies/base.lock.json
Uploading policy base (6743503767) to policy group production
Uploaded docker      4.8.0 (d074b095)
Uploaded dockerhost 0.1.0 (3f2a6710)
```

2. Next, we will assign all our Docker hosts to the `production` policy group and the policy `base` that we uploaded earlier:

```
$ knife node policy set dockerhost production base
Successfully set the policy on node dockerhost
$ knife node policy set node1 production base
Successfully set the policy on node node1
```

3. Finally, we will run the `chef-client` on both our Docker hosts. The `chef-client` will fetch and apply the desired state configuration we applied in the previous steps:

```
$ knife ssh 'policy_group:production' 'chef-client'
node1      Starting Chef Client, version 14.7.17
dockerhost Starting Chef Client, version 14.7.17
node1      Using policy 'base' at revision...
dockerhost Using policy 'base' at revision...
...
node1              * service[docker] action start dockerhost        *
service[docker] action start
node1
node1      Running handlers:
node1      Running handlers complete
node1      Chef Client finished, ... in 53 seconds
dockerhost
dockerhost Running handlers:
dockerhost Running handlers complete
dockerhost Chef Client finished, ... in 53 seconds
```

Now, we have Docker installed and configured in our Docker host using Chef. Whenever we need to add another Docker host, we can just create another server in our cloud provider and assign it to our `production` policy group and policy `base`.

In a production environment, the goal of having configuration management software installed in our Docker host is never to have the need to log in to it just to perform configuration updates. Running the `chef-client` manually is only half the automation.

We will want to run the `chef-client` as a daemon process so that we don't have to run it every time we perform an update. The `chef-client` daemon will poll the Chef server to check whether there are any updates to the node it is managing. By default, this polling interval is set to 30 minutes.
For more information on how to configure the `chef-client` as a daemon, refer to the Chef documentation at `https://docs.chef.io/chef_client.html`.

In the next section, we will iterate on our Chef cookbook to include the initialization of our Docker Swarm cluster.

Initializing Docker Swarm

Now that we have a base configuration of setting up a Docker host, let us move to the next level and set up a Docker Swarm cluster automatically:

1. First, we need a way to store the Docker Swarm join token securely. We will use `chef-vault` as a way to store the token. To be able to use `chef-vault`, we will simply add it as a dependency of our cookbook in `cookbooks/dockerhost/metadata.rb`:

   ```
   name 'dockerhost'
   # ...
   version '0.1.0'

   depends 'docker', '~> 4.7'
   depends 'chef-vault', '~> 3.1' # update here
   ```

2. Next, we will create a Chef recipe for initializing the manager node in `cookbooks/dockerhost/recipes/manager.rb`:

   ```
   include_recipe 'dockerhost::base'

   execute 'init swarm' do
     command 'docker swarm init'
     not_if 'docker info -f "{{.Swarm.LocalNodeState}}" | egrep
   "^active"'
   end
   ```

   Note that we used Chef's guard clauses to prevent `docker swarm init` from running multiple times. This makes our Chef recipe idempotent.

3. Back in our base recipe, `cookbooks/dockerhost/recipes/base.rb`, we will grab the join token from `chef-vault` and run `docker join` with it:

   ```
   # previous contents of
   # cookbooks/dockerhost/recipes/base.rb
   # ...

   swarm = begin
             chef_vault_item('docker', 'swarm')\
               [node.policy_group]
           rescue Net::HTTPServerException
             {}
           end
   ```

```
execute 'join swarm' do
  command 'docker swarm join '\
          "--token #{swarm['token']} #{swarm['manager']}"
  not_if { swarm.empty? }
  not_if 'docker info -f "{{.Swarm.LocalNodeState}}" | egrep
"^active"'
end
```

4. Next, we will tie all our changes by updating our Chef Policyfile
   `policies/base.rb`:

   ```
   name 'base'

   default_source :supermarket
   cookbook 'dockerhost', path: '../cookbooks/dockerhost'

   run_list 'dockerhost::base'
   named_run_list 'manager', 'dockerhost::manager'
   ```

5. Once everything is updated, we will update the policy to generate a new lock
   file:

   ```
   $ chef update policies/base.rb
   Building policy base
   Expanded run list: recipe[dockerhost::base]
   Caching Cookbooks...
   Installing dockerhost >= 0.0.0 from path
   Using        docker     4.8.0
   Installing chef-vault 3.1.1

   Lockfile written to ./policies/base.lock.json
   Policy revision id: 9f698c0ddb57b3dcc6af62406588c3
   ```

6. Finally, let us now push this new policy to our Chef server:

   ```
   $ chef push production policies/base.lock.json
   ```

Now that we have updated our policy, we can now apply it again to our Docker hosts. The
next few steps will initialize our Docker Swarm cluster:

1. First, we run the manager recipe that we created earlier in our Docker host
   `dockerhost`:

   ```
   $ knife ssh -m dockerhost 'chef-client --named-run-list manager'
   dockerhost Starting Chef Client, version 14.7.17
   ...
   dockerhost    * execute[join swarm] action run (skipped due to
   ```

```
not_if)
dockerhost Recipe: dockerhost::manager
dockerhost   * execute[init swarm] action run
dockerhost      - execute docker swarm init
dockerhost
dockerhost Running handlers:
dockerhost Running handlers complete
dockerhost Chef Client finished, ... in 09 seconds
```

2. Next, we will log in to this Docker host to grab the join token:

```
$ knife ssh -m dockerhost 'docker swarm join-token worker'
dockerhost To add a worker to this swarm, run the following
command:
dockerhost
dockerhost
docker swarm join --token SWMTKN-1-31h15evixetseazrs...
172.16.132.218:2377
dockerhost
```

3. Now that we know what the join token is, we will use this information to create a
   chef-vault item file in vault/docker/swarm.json:

```
{
  "production": {
    "token": "SWMTKN-1-31h15evixetseazrs...",
    "manager": "172.16.132.218:2377"
  }
}
```

4. Next, we will upload this chef-vault item by running the following command:

```
$ knife vault create -m client \
    docker swarm "$(cat vault/docker/swarm.json) \
    -S 'policy_group:production'
```

5. Finally, we will run Chef again in all our Docker hosts:

```
$ knife ssh 'policy_group:production' 'chef-client'
dockerhost Starting Chef Client, version 14.7.17
node1      Starting Chef Client, version 14.7.17
. . .
dockerhost   * execute[join swarm] action run (skipped...)
node1        * execute[join swarm] action run
node1          - execute docker swarm join --token ...
dockerhost
dockerhost Running handlers:
dockerhost Running handlers complete
```

```
dockerhost Chef Client finished, ... in 09 seconds
node1
node1        Running handlers:
node1        Running handlers complete
node1        Chef Client finished, ... in 10 seconds
```

As we can see in the preceding snippet, `node1` joined our Docker Swarm cluster. Our manager node `dockerhost` didn't reinitialize the swarm because it is already part of the cluster.

We are now done setting up our Docker Swarm cluster as we did in the previous chapter. But now we have automated most of the steps in setting it up.

 We can use `chef-vault` as well for distributing the Docker Swarm manager's TLS keys and certificates in a similar fashion.

Alternative methods

There are other general-purpose configuration management tools that allow us to configure our Docker host. The following is a short list of the other tools that we can use:

- **Puppet**: Refer to `http://puppetlabs.com`.
- **Ansible**: This can be found at `http://ansible.com`.
- **CFEngine**: This is available at `http://cfengine.com`.
- **SaltStack**: You can find more on this at `http://saltstack.com`.
- **Docker Machine**: This is a very specific configuration management tool that allows us to provision and configure Docker hosts in our infrastructure. More information about Docker Machine can be found on the Docker documentation page at `https://docs.docker.com/machine`.

If we do not want to manage our Docker host infrastructure at all, we can use Docker hosting services. Popular cloud providers started offering Docker hosts as a preprovisioned cloud image that we can use. Others offer a more comprehensive solution that allows us to interact with all the Docker hosts in the cloud as a single virtual Docker host. The following is a list of links of the popular cloud providers describing their integration with the Docker ecosystem:

- Google Kubernetes Engine (`https://cloud.google.com/kubernetes-engine`)
- Amazon EC2 Container Service (`http://aws.amazon.com/documentation/ecs`)
- Azure Container Instances (`https://azure.microsoft.com/en-us/services/container-instances/`)
- Joyent Triton Compute (`https://www.joyent.com/triton/compute`)

In terms of deploying Docker containers, there are several container tools that allow you to do this. They provide APIs to run and deploy our Docker containers. Some of the offered APIs are even compatible with the Docker engine itself. This allows us to interact with our pool of Docker hosts as if it is a single virtual Docker host. The following is a list of a few tools that allow us to orchestrate the deployment of our containers to a pool of Docker hosts:

- CNCF Kubernetes (`http://kubernetes.io`)
- Mesophere Marathon (`https://mesosphere.github.io/marathon`)
- SmartDataCenter Docker Engine (`https://github.com/joyent/sdc-docker`)

However, we still need configuration management tools such as Chef to deploy and configure our orchestration systems at the top of our pool of Docker hosts.

Summary

In this chapter, we learned how to automate the configuration of our Docker deployments. Using Chef allows us to configure and provision multiple Docker hosts in scale. From this point on, we can write Chef recipes to persist all the Docker optimization techniques we will learn in this book.

In the next chapter, we will introduce instrumentation to monitor our whole Docker infrastructure and application. This will give us further feedback on how to optimize our Docker deployments better for higher performance.

Monitoring Docker

3

We now know some ways to optimize our Docker deployments. We also know how to scale to improve performance. But how do we know that our tuning assumptions were correct? Being able to monitor our Docker infrastructure and application is important to figure out why and when we need to optimize. Measuring how our system is performing allows us to identify its limits in order to scale and tune accordingly.

In addition to monitoring low-level information about Docker, it is also important to measure the business-related performance of our application. By tracing the value stream of our application, we can correlate business-related metrics to system-level ones. With this, our Docker development and operations teams can show their business colleagues how Docker reduces their organization's costs and increases business value.

In this chapter, we will cover the following topics concerning our ability to monitor our Docker infrastructure and applications at scale:

- The importance of monitoring
- Collecting metrics in Prometheus
- Consolidating logs in an ELK stack

The importance of monitoring

Monitoring is important as it provides a source of feedback on the Docker deployment that we built. It provides an in-depth view of our application, from the performance of the low-level operating system to high-level business targets. Having proper instrumentation inserted in our Docker hosts allows us to identify our system's state. We can use this source of feedback to identify whether our application is behaving as originally planned.

If our initial hypothesis was incorrect, we can use the feedback data to revise our plan and change our system accordingly by tuning our Docker host and containers or updating our running Docker application. We can also use the same monitoring process to identify errors and bugs after our system is deployed to production.

Docker has built-in features to log and monitor. By default, a Docker host stores a Docker container's standard output and error streams to JSON files in `/var/lib/docker/<container_id>/<container_id>-json.log`. The `docker logs` command asks the Docker Engine daemon to read the contents of the files here.

Another monitoring facility is the `docker stats` command. This queries the Docker Engine's remote API's `/containers/<container_id>/stats` endpoint to report runtime statistics about the running container's control group regarding its CPU, memory, and network usage. The following is an example output of the `docker stats` command reporting these metrics:

```
dockerhost$ docker run --name running -d busybox \
    /bin/sh -c 'while true; do echo hello && sleep 1; done'
dockerhost$ docker stats running
CONTAINER      CPU %     MEM USAGE/LIMIT   MEM %      NET I/O
running        0.00%     0 B/518.5 MB      0.00%      17.06 MB/119.8 kB
```

The built-in `docker logs` and `docker stats` commands work well to monitor our Docker applications for development and small-scale deployments. When we get to a point in our production-grade Docker deployment where we manage tens, hundreds, or even thousands of Docker hosts, this approach will no longer be scalable. It is not feasible to log in to each of our thousand Docker hosts and type `docker logs` and `docker stats`.

Doing this one by one also makes it difficult to create a more holistic picture of our entire Docker deployment. Also, not everyone who is interested in our Docker application's performance can log in to our Docker hosts. Colleagues dealing with only the business aspect of our application may want to ask certain questions concerning how our application's deployment in Docker improves what our organization wants; however, they do not necessarily want to learn how to log in and start typing Docker commands in our infrastructure.

Therefore, it is important to be able to consolidate all of the events and metrics from our Docker deployments into a centralized monitoring infrastructure. This allows our operations to scale by having a single point from which we can find out what is happening to our system. A centralized dashboard also enables people outside our development and operations team, such as our business colleagues, to have access to the feedback provided by our monitoring system. The remaining sections will show you how to consolidate messages from `docker logs` and collect statistics from data sources, such as `docker stats`.

Collecting metrics with Prometheus

To begin monitoring our Docker deployments, we must first set up an endpoint to send our monitored values to. Prometheus is a popular monitoring stack for collecting various metrics. It provides a simple API for integration with various tools. Most cloud-native and container-related tools already support integration with Prometheus. Later, we will configure Prometheus to collect metrics from our Docker infrastructure.

In this section, we will set up the following components to build our monitoring infrastructure based on Prometheus:

- **Prometheus clients/exporters**: These are basically any kind of component that uses Prometheus's exposition format that exposes metrics to be collected by Prometheus. We will activate Prometheus's integration with Docker Engine to monitor Docker-related metrics in our cluster. We will also deploy cAdvisor, a tool to monitor containers that are running in all our Docker Swarm nodes.
- **Prometheus**: We will configure Prometheus itself to scrape and gather metrics from the various client/exporters we have set up.
- **Grafana**: Grafana provides a nice visualization for various metric storage engines. Although Prometheus provides some basic graphing out of the box, Grafana has a nicer interface for visualizing the metrics that we will gather. We will configure Grafana to connect to our Prometheus service and inspect the containers running inside our Docker Swarm cluster.

Exposing Prometheus's metrics

To start monitoring our Docker infrastructure, we need to expose metrics from the nodes in our Docker Swarm cluster. By the end of this section, we will get Prometheus-compatible metrics from the following components:

- **Docker Engine**: Provides Prometheus integration that is built in to the Docker Engine itself
- **cAdvisor**: A tool from Google that monitors all containers running in a machine. It provides integration with Docker out of the box

First, we need to update the Docker Engine daemon running in each of our nodes. The following steps illustrate how to perform this update:

1. First, let's go back to our Chef cookbook that we wrote in the previous chapter. Let's update our Chef recipe in `cookbooks/dockerhost/recipes/base.rb` using the following code:

```
# cookbooks/dockerhost/recipes/base.rb
# ...

docker_service 'default' do
  misc_opts '--experimental=true --metrics-addr=0.0.0.0:1337'
  # ...
end

# ...
```

   In the preceding code, we enabled Prometheus to integrate with the Docker Engine by specifying the `--metrics-addr` flag. At this time, it is still an experimental feature of Docker, so we also need to set the `--experimental` flag as well.

2. Now that we have edited our cookbook, let's now update our Chef policy and push it to our Chef server, as follows:

```
$ chef update policies/base.rb
$ chef push production policies/base.lock.json
```

3. Finally, let's run the `chef-client` in all our nodes, as follows. This will restart all the Docker Engine daemons to pick up the updated configuration:

```
$ knife ssh policy_group:production 'sudo chef-client'
```

Our Prometheus metrics are exposed. We can test this by querying the Prometheus endpoints of each of our Docker nodes by hand, as follows:

```
$ curl http://dockerhost:1337/metrics
...
$ curl http://node1:1337/metrics
...
swarm_store_write_tx_latency_seconds_bucket{le="2.5"} 0
swarm_store_write_tx_latency_seconds_bucket{le="5"} 0
swarm_store_write_tx_latency_seconds_bucket{le="10"} 0
swarm_store_write_tx_latency_seconds_bucket{le="+Inf"} 0
swarm_store_write_tx_latency_seconds_sum 0
swarm_store_write_tx_latency_seconds_count 0
```

At the time of writing, the Prometheus integration in Docker only supports exposing metrics for the Docker Engine itself. In order to collect the actual metrics from our running containers on each host, we will need to install Google's cAdvisor.

The next few steps will deploy cAdvisor to all of the nodes participating in our Docker Swarm cluster:

1. First, we will create a Docker Compose YAML file called compose-monitoring.yml to describe how to run the cAdvisor service, as follows:

```
---
version: '3.7'

services:
  cadvisor:
    image: google/cadvisor
    hostname: '{{.Node.Hostname}}'
    deploy:
      mode: global
    command: -logtostderr=true -docker_only=true
    volumes:
      - /:/rootfs:ro
      - /var/run:/var/run:rw
      - /sys:/sys:ro
      - /var/lib/docker:/var/lib/docker:ro

# Set for debugging and testing purposes
networks:
  default:
    driver: overlay
    attachable: true
```

The important aspect of this service definition is the `deploy/mode: global` entry. A global service will run cAdvisor containers on every node in our Docker Swarm cluster. This includes the manager nodes as well.

2. After creating the Compose YAML file, let's now deploy it to our Docker Swarm cluster, as follows:

```
$ docker stack deploy -c compose-monitoring.yml monitoring
Creating network monitoring_default
Creating service monitoring_cadvisor
```

3. We can now test whether cAdvisor is exposing container metrics by contacting the running Docker service, as follows:

```
$ docker run --network monitoring_default -it --rm alpine /bin/sh
/ # apk add -y curl
/ # curl http://cadvisor:8080/metrics
. . .
# HELP process_start_time_seconds Start time of the process since
unix epoch in seconds.
# TYPE process_start_time_seconds gauge
process_start_time_seconds 1.54791282078e+09
# HELP process_virtual_memory_bytes Virtual memory size in bytes.
# TYPE process_virtual_memory_bytes gauge
process_virtual_memory_bytes 7.63068416e+0
```

We now have processes that expose Prometheus metrics for our containers. You can use the following references to learn more about these tools:

- **Docker**: https://docs.docker.com/config/thirdparty/prometheus
- **cAdvisor**: https://github.com/google/cadvisor

Scraping and visualizing metrics

Now that all the Prometheus endpoints are prepared, we can now proceed with collecting these metrics in Prometheus itself. Afterwards, we will run Grafana to visualize all of the metrics that we have exposed in the previous subsection.

The following steps will deploy Prometheus as a service in our Docker Swarm cluster:

1. First, let's prepare a service config for Prometheus in a file called
   `prometheus.yml`, as follows:

```
---
global:
  scrape_interval: 15s

scrape_configs:
  - job_name: cadvisor
    dns_sd_configs:
      - names:
          - 'tasks.cadvisor'
        type: A
        port: 8080
  - job_name: docker
    static_configs:
      - targets:
          - dockerhost:1337
          - node1:1337
```

In the preceding configuration, we scraped each Docker Engine in our Docker Swarm cluster by specifying the hostname of each node. For cAdvisor, we used Prometheus's built-in service discovery via DNS to connect to all the cAdvisor containers running in each node.

2. To start Prometheus, let's update our `compose-monitoring.yml` file with the following entry:

```
---
version: '3.7'

services:
  prometheus:
    image: prom/prometheus
    configs:
      - source: prometheus.yml
        target: /etc/prometheus/prometheus.yml
# ...   cadvisor:

configs:
  prometheus.yml:
    file: ./prometheus.yml

# networks ...
```

In the preceding update, we made sure that the service config is properly referenced.

3. Finally, let's update the deployment of our monitoring services stack, as follows:

```
$ docker stack deploy -c compose-monitoring.yml monitoring
Creating config monitoring_prometheus.yml
Creating service monitoring_prometheus
Updating service monitoring_cadvisor (id: eiqb0w6e86bjm596vsut377)
```

Prometheus is now ready, and is scraping the metric endpoints we configured earlier. Let's confirm that all the endpoints are being scraped properly by querying the target API's endpoint of our Prometheus service, as follows:

```
$ docker run --network monitoring_default -it --rm alpine /bin/sh
/ # apk add -y curl jq
/ # curl -s http://prometheus:9090/api/v1/targets   \
| jq '.data.activeTargets | .[].labels'
{
  "instance": "10.0.4.3:8080",
  "job": "cadvisor"
}
{
  "instance": "10.0.4.4:8080",
  "job": "cadvisor"
}
{
  "instance": "dockerhost:1337",
  "job": "docker"
}
{
  "instance": "node1:1337",
  "job": "docker"
}
```

The next component in our monitoring stack is Grafana. The following steps will deploy Grafana as a service in our Docker Swarm cluster:

1. First, let's update the Docker Compose file named `compose-logging.yml` to define how Grafana will run in our cluster, as follows:

```
---
version: '3.7'

services:
  grafana:
    image: grafana/grafana
```

```
      ports:
        - 3000:3000
# prometheus:
# cadvisor:
# ...
```

2. Now that we've finished updating the Compose file, let's perform a redeployment using the following command:

```
$ docker stack deploy -c compose-monitoring.yml monitoring
Creating service monitoring_grafana
Updating service monitoring_prometheus (id:
hzarfvo8kd9g6cj441n31db7g)
Updating service monitoring_cadvisor (id:
eiqb0w6e86bjm596vsut377ws)
```

3. Grafana should now be ready. Since we set up an ingress port for Docker Swarm's routing mesh, we can go to `http://dockerhost:3000` to visit our Grafana deployment.

4. When we first bring up Grafana, we will be asked to log in. Let's use the default username admin and password admin configured in the official Grafana container, as shown in the following screenshot:

Although optional, let us change the default administrator password of our Grafana installation as well:

1. At the main dashboard, the Grafana installation tells us what to do first, which is to add a datasource. In the configuration page (as shown in the following screenshot), we will be inserting a Prometheus data source type:

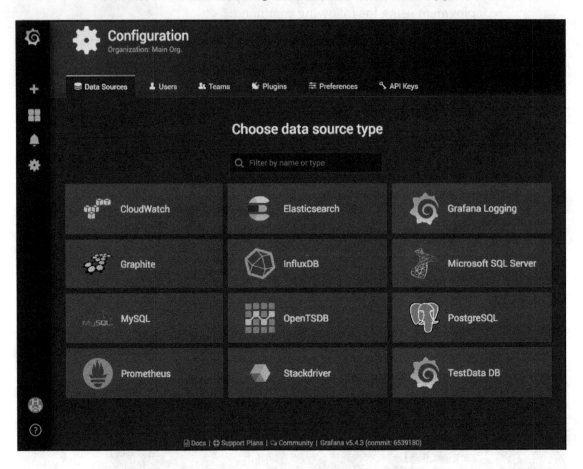

2. To configure Grafana to query our Prometheus service, let's set the HTTP URL at `http://prometheus:9090`, as shown in the following screenshot. This is where the service is located based on the definition of our Docker Compose file:

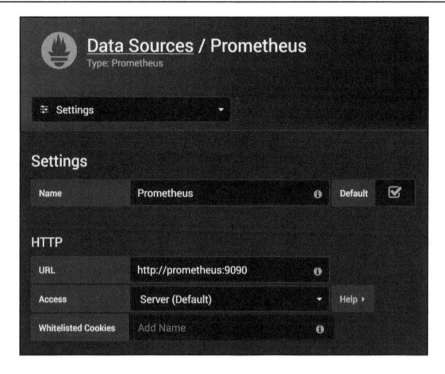

3. To update the changes, let's go all the way down the page and press the **Save & Test** button.

4. We are now ready to visualize container metrics in our Docker Swarm cluster.

5. Let's go to the dashboard search area of Grafana and click on **Import dashboard**. Let's paste the following text into the **JSON** textbox:

```
{
  "panels": [
    {
      "id": 2,
      "stack": true,
      "targets": [
        {
          "expr":        "rate(container_cpu_usage_seconds_total
{container_label_com_docker_stack_namespace=\"monitoring\"}[1m])",
          "legendFormat": "{{name}}"
        }
      ],
      "title": "Container CPU usage",
      "type": "graph"
    }
  ],
```

```
        "title": "Docker Monitoring"
}
```

We may need to adjust the size of the graphed area in our dashboard as necessary to see the visualization properly.

Once the dashboard is imported, we will see the CPU usage of the monitoring stack we just deployed in this section. The dashboard will look something like the following screenshot:

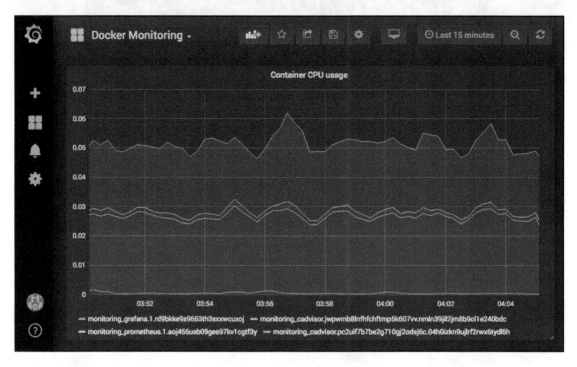

Congratulations! We now have a proper monitoring stack for our Docker Swarm cluster.

Consolidating logs in an ELK stack

Not all statuses of our Docker hosts and containers are readily available to be queried with our monitoring solution in Prometheus. Some events and metrics are only available as raw lines of text in log files. We need to transform these raw and unstructured logs to meaningful metrics. Similar to raw metrics, we can later ask higher-level questions about what is happening in our Docker-based application using analytics.

The ELK stack is a popular combination suite from Elastic that addresses these problems. Each letter in the acronym represents each of its components. The following list contains descriptions of each of them:

- **Elasticsearch**: Elasticsearch is a distributed search engine that is highly scalable. Its sharding capabilities allow us to grow and scale our log storage as we continue to receive more and more logs from our Docker containers. Its database engine is document oriented. This allows us to store and annotate logs as we see fit as we continue to discover more insights about the events we are managing in our large Docker deployments.
- **Logstash**: Logstash is the component that is used to collect and manage logs and events. It is the central point that we use to collect all the logs from different log sources, such as multiple Docker hosts and containers running in our deployment. We can also use Logstash to transform and annotate the logs we receive. This allows us to search and explore the richer features of our logs later.
- **Kibana**: Kibana is an analytics and search dashboard for Elasticsearch. Its simplicity allows us to create dashboards for our Docker applications; however, Kibana is also very flexible to customize, so we can build dashboards that can provide valuable insights to people who want to understand our Docker-based applications, whether they have a low-level, technical detail or higher-level business need.

In the remaining parts of this section, we will set up each of these components and send our Docker host and container logs to them.

Deploying Elasticsearch, Logstash, and Kibana

We will set up the ELK stack by creating a Docker Compose file to describe these services. The next few steps describe how to build the ELK stack:

1. First, let's deploy the Elasticsearch service by creating the file called `compose-logging.yml`, as shown in the following code:

   ```
   ---
   version: '3.7'

   services:
     elasticsearch:
       image: elasticsearch:6.5.4
       environment:
         discovery.type: single-node
   ```

```
      networks:
        default:
          driver: overlay
          attachable: true
```

2. Next, we deploy this Docker Compose file and do a quick test to confirm that Elasticsearch is running using the following code. Depending on the capacity of our Docker host, it may take a while for Elasticsearch to be ready:

```
$ docker stack deploy -c compose-logging.yml logging
Creating network logging_default
Creating service logging_elasticsearch
$ docker run --network logging_default -it --rm alpine /bin/sh
/ # apk add curl
/ # curl http://elasticsearch:9200/_cluster/health\?pretty=true
{
  "cluster_name" : "docker-cluster",
  "status" : "green",
  "timed_out" : false,
  "number_of_nodes" : 1,
...
}
```

3. Next, we will update the `compose-logging.yml` file to launch Kibana, as follows:

```
---
version: '3.7'

services:
  kibana:
    image: kibana:6.5.4
    ports:
      - 5601:5601
#  elasticsearch: ...

# networks: ...
```

4. After the new Docker Compose file is ready, launch Kibana by rerunning the stack deployment as follows:

```
$ docker stack deploy -c compose-logging.yml logging
Creating service logging_kibana
Updating service logging_elasticsearch (id:\
1ewcnk24h7xdc3obwd7nwy9nm)
```

5. Since we enabled the Docker Swarm ingress port for Kibana, we can visit `http://dockerhost:5601` to see whether our Kibana service is running. We should see a welcome page like the one in the following screenshot:

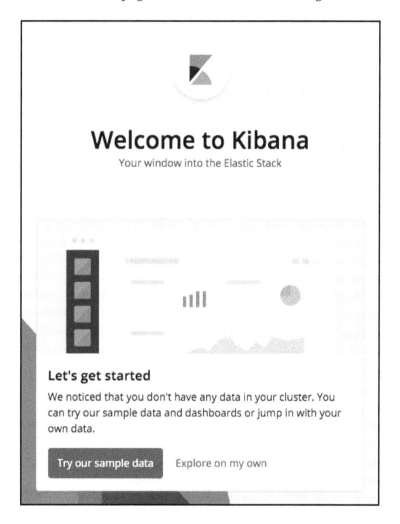

We will look at creating a dashboard from Elasticsearch data in the next section:

1. To create the last part of our logging stack, we first need to create a configuration file named `logstash.conf` for Logstash, as follows:

```
input {
  gelf { }
}
```

```
output {
  # Optional: Enable for debugging
  # stdout { }
  elasticsearch {
    hosts => ["http://elasticsearch:9200"]
  }
}
```

2. Next, we update the `compose-logging.yml` file by defining how the Logstash service will run using the following code. Note that we also include the `logstash.conf` file that we prepared in the previous step:

```
---
version: '3.7'

services:
#  kibana: ...
#  elasticsearch: ...
  logstash:
    configs:
      - source: logstash.conf
        target: /usr/share/logstash/pipeline/logstash.conf
    image: logstash:6.5.4
    ports:
      - 12201:12201/udp

configs:
  logstash.conf:
    file: ./logstash.conf

# networks: ...
```

3. Finally, we deploy Logstash and confirm that it is working by using the following code:

```
$ docker stack deploy -c compose-logging.yml logging
Creating config logging_logstash.conf
Updating service logging_kibana (id: 1utcs8yl6k3zavdrms8q7vccm)
Updating service logging_elasticsearch (id:\
1ewcnk24h7xdc3obwd7nwy9nm)
Creating service logging_logstash
$ docker run --network logging_default -it --rm alpine /bin/sh
/ # apk add curl
/ # curl http://logstash:9600/\?pretty
{
 "host" : "3645f635a7b8",
 "version" : "6.5.4",
 "http_address" : "0.0.0.0:9600",
```

```
    "id" : "704b7fa5-1286-49ed-8381-f5ed79eb109d",
    "name" : "3645f635a7b8",
    "build_date" : "2018-12-17T22:04:46+00:00",
    "build_sha" : "7bf353ed88a10f3f2a9b81f6f3510ee41061e2f8",
    "build_snapshot" : false
}/
```

We now have the entire stack of our logging infrastructure in place. Now we need to configure our Docker Swarm cluster to send logs to this stack's services.

Forwarding Docker container logs

Now that we have a basic functional ELK stack, we can start forwarding our Docker logs to it. Support for custom logging drivers has been available from Docker 1.7 onward. In this section, we will configure our Docker host to use the GELF driver. Let's go through the following steps to start receiving our container logs in the ELK stack:

1. Update the base.rb recipe as follows:

   ```
   # cookbooks/dockerhost/recipes/base.rb
   # ...

   docker_service 'default' do
     log_driver 'gelf'
     log_opts "gelf-address=udp://#{node['ipaddress']}:12201"
     # misc_opts ... (for metrics in the previous section)
     # ...
   end

   # ...
   ```

2. Update the policy and deploy it using the following code:

   ```
   $ chef update policies/base.rb
   $ chef push production policies/base.lock.json
   ```

3. Run chef-client in the Docker Swarm nodes, as follows:

   ```
   $ knife ssh policy_group:production 'sudo chef-client'
   ```

Any standard output and error streams coming out from our Docker container should now be captured and placed in our ELK stack. We can do some preliminary tests to confirm that the setup works. Type the following command to create a test message from Docker:

```
$ docker run --rm busybox echo message to elk
```

The `docker run` command also supports the `--log-driver` and `--log-opt=[]` command-line options to set up the logging driver only for the container we want to run. We can use it to further tune our logging policies for each Docker container running in our Docker host.

In the next few steps, we will perform some minimal setup in Kibana so that we can search for the log message that we sent from Docker earlier:

1. First, we need to create an index pattern where Kibana will look for Elasticsearch logs. Let's go to `http://dockerhost:5601/app/kibana#/management/kibana/index` and use the default indices generated by Logstash `logstash-*` as our index pattern, as shown in the following screenshot:

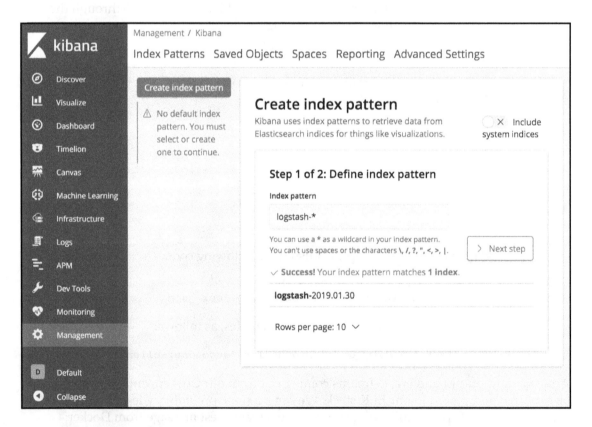

Let's click on **Next step** to proceed to the next configuration dialogs.

2. Now that we have an index pattern, we need to indicate which fields in the index documents contain the timestamp of our logs. Let's use the default timefield `@timestamp`, as follows:

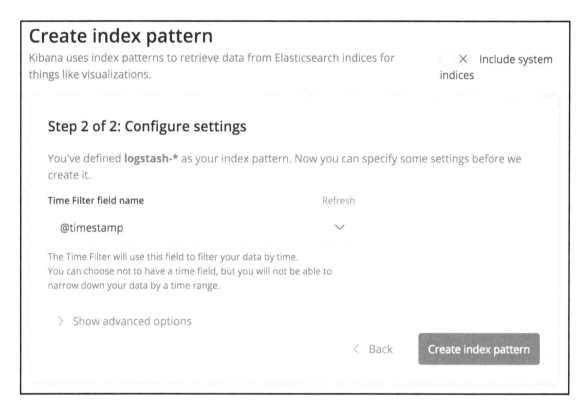

3. Finally, let's click on the **Create index pattern** button to finish the creation of our index pattern.

Kibana is now configured to look at our Docker logs. Let's go to our Kibana endpoint in `http://dockerhost:5601/app/kibana#/discover` and search for the phrase `"message to elk"` (including the quotation marks) in the textbox. The search result should give the entry for the message we sent earlier. The following screenshot is what the search result should look like:

In the preceding screenshot, we can see the message we sent. There is also other information about the container that generated the log message. Docker's GELF log driver contains information such as the source Docker image name, container identification, and the Docker host where the container was run.

 Aside from the GELF and default JSON file logging drivers, Docker supports several other endpoints to send logs to. More information about all the logging drivers and their respective usage guides can be found at `https://docs.docker.com/config/containers/logging/`.

Other monitoring and logging solutions

There are several other solutions that we can use to monitor and log infrastructure in order to support our Docker-based application. Some of them already have built-in support for monitoring Docker containers. Others should be combined with other solutions, such as the ones we saw previously, because they only focus on a specific part of monitoring or logging.

With other solutions, we may have to use some workarounds; however, their benefits clearly outweigh the compromise we have to make. While the following list is not exhaustive, it shows a few of the stacks we can explore to create our logging and monitoring solutions:

- Graphite (`http://graphiteapp.org/`)
- InfluxDB (`http://influxdb.com`)
- Sensu (`http://sensuapp.org`)
- Fluentd (`http://www.fluentd.org/`)
- Graylog (`http://www.graylog.org`)
- Splunk (`http://www.splunk.com`)

Sometimes, the operations staff and developers running and developing our Docker applications are not yet mature enough or do not want to focus on maintaining such monitoring and logging infrastructures. There are several hosted monitoring and logging platforms that we can use so that we can focus on actually writing and improving the performance of our Docker application.

Some of them work with existing monitoring and logging agents. With others, we may have to download and deploy their agents to be able to forward the events and metrics to their hosted platform. The following is a non exhaustive list of some solutions that we may want to consider:

- New Relic (http://www.newrelic.com)
- Datadog (http://www.datadoghq.com)
- Librato (http://www.librato.com)
- Elastic Cloud (http://www.elastic.co/cloud)
- Treasure Data (http://www.treasuredata.com)
- Splunk Cloud (http://www.splunk.com)

Summary

We now know why it is important to monitor our Docker deployments in a scalable and accessible manner. We deployed Prometheus to monitor our Docker container's metrics. We rolled out an ELK stack to consolidate the logs coming from various Docker hosts and containers.

In addition to raw metrics and events, it is also important to know what it means for our application. Grafana and Kibana allow us to create custom dashboards and analysis to provide insight into our Docker applications. With these monitoring tools and skills in our arsenal, we should be able to operate and run our Docker deployments well in production.

In the next chapter, we will be optimizing our Docker images and improving our development workflow.

4
Optimizing Docker Images

Docker images provide a standard package format that lets developers and system administrators work together to simplify the management of an application's code. Docker's container format allows us to rapidly iterate the versions of our application and share them with the rest of our organization. Our development, testing, and deployment time are shorter than they would otherwise be because of the lightweight feature and speed of Docker containers. The portability of Docker containers allows us to scale our applications from physical servers to virtual machines in the cloud.

However, we will start noticing that the same reasons for which we used Docker in the first place are losing their beneficial effects. Development time is increasing because we always have to download the newest version of our application's Docker image runtime library. Deployment takes a lot more time because Docker Hub is slow; at worst, Docker Hub may be down, and we won't be able to do any deployment at all. Our Docker images are now so big, in the order of gigabytes, that simple single-line updates take the whole day.

This chapter will cover the following scenarios of how Docker containers get out of hand and suggests steps to remediate the problems mentioned earlier:

- Reducing image deployment time
- Improving image build time
- Reducing Docker image size
- Guide to optimization

After this chapter, we will have a more streamlined build and deploy workflow of our Docker images.

Reducing deployment time

As time goes by while we build our Docker container, its size will get bigger and bigger. Updating running containers in our existing Docker hosts is not a problem. Docker takes advantage of the Docker image layers that we build over time as our application grows; however, consider the case where we want to scale out our application. This requires deploying more Docker containers to additional Docker hosts. In this case, each new Docker host will have to download all of the large image layers that we built over time. This section will show you how a large Docker application affects deployment time on new Docker hosts. First, let's build this problematic Docker application by carrying out the following steps:

1. Write the following Dockerfile to create our large Docker image:

   ```
   FROM debian:stretch

   RUN dd if=/dev/urandom of=/largefile bs=1024 count=524288
   ```

2. Next, build the Dockerfile as `hubuser/largeapp` using the following command:

   ```
   dockerhost$ docker build -t hubuser/largeapp .
   ```

3. Take note of how large the created Docker image is. In the following example output, the size is `662 MB`:

   ```
   dockerhost$ docker images
   REPOSITORY              TAG        IMAGE ID        CREATED         SIZE
   aespinosa/largeapp latest         0e519ec6e31f    2 minutes ago   637MB
   debian                  stretch    d508d16c64cd    2 days ago      101MB
   ```

4. Using the `time` command, record how long it takes to push and pull it from Docker Hub, as follows:

   ```
   dockerhost$ time docker push hubuser/largeapp
   The push refers to repository [docker.io/hubuser/largeapp]
   eb6ed1590bf8: Pushed
   13d5529fd232: Layer already exists
   latest: digest:
   sha256:0ff29cc728fc8c274bc0ac43ca2815986ced89fbff35399b1c0e7d4bf31c
   size: 742
   real    11m34.133s
   user    0m0.164s
   sys     0m0.104s
   ```

5. Let's also do the same timing test when pulling the Docker image, but let's now delete the image from our Docker daemon first, as shown in the following code:

```
dockerhost$ docker rmi hubuser/largeapp
dockerhost$ time docker pull hubuser/largeapp
Using default tag: latest
latest: Pulling from hubuser/largeapp
741437d97401: Pull complete
d7d6d7c9ffc5: Pull complete
Digest:
sha256:0ff29cc728fc8c274bc0ac43ca2815986ced89fbff35399b1c0e7d4bf31c
Status: Downloaded newer image for hubuser/largeapp:latest
real    2m19.909s
user    0m0.707s
sys     0m0.645s
```

As we can see in the timing results, it takes a lot of time to use `docker push` to upload an image to Docker Hub. Upon deployment, `docker pull` takes just as long to propagate our newly created Docker image to our new production Docker hosts. These upload and download time values also depend on the network connection between Docker Hub and our Docker hosts. Ultimately, when Docker Hub goes down, we will lose the ability to deploy new Docker containers or scale out to additional Docker hosts on demand.

In order to take advantage of Docker's fast delivery of applications and ease of deployment and scaling, it is important that our method of pushing and pulling Docker images is reliable and fast. Fortunately, we can run our own Docker registry so that it can host and distribute our Docker images without relying on the public Docker Hub. The next few steps describe how to set this up to confirm the improvement in performance:

1. Let's run our own Docker registry by typing the following command. This code is for a local registry running at `tcp://dockerhost:5000`:

```
dockerhost$ docker run --network=host -d registry:2
```

2. Next, let's confirm how our Docker image deployments have improved. First, create a tag for the image we created earlier in order to push it to the local Docker registry using the following:

```
dockerhost$ docker tag hubuser/largeapp dockerhost:5000/largeapp
```

3. Observe how much faster it is to push the same Docker image over our newly running Docker registry. The following tests show that pushing Docker images is now at least 10 times faster:

```
dockerhost$ docker push dockerhost:5000/largeapp
The push refers to repository [dockerhost:5000/largeapp]
latest: digest:
sha256:0ff29cc728fc8c274bc0ac43ca2815986ced89fbff35399b1c0e7d4bf...
size: 742
real    0m46.816s
user    0m0.090s
sys     0m0.064s
```

4. Now, confirm the new performance when we pull our Docker images from our local Docker registry. The following tests show that the downloading of Docker images is now several orders of magnitude faster:

```
# make sure we removed the image we built
dockerhost$ docker rmi dockerhost:5000/largeapp hubuser/largeapp
dockerhost$ time docker pull dockerhost:5000/largeapp
Using default tag: latest
latest: Pulling from largeapp
Digest:
sha256:0ff29cc728fc8c274bc0ac43ca2815986ced89fbff35399b1c0e7d4bf31c
38e1
Status: Downloaded newer image for dockerhost:5000/largeapp:latest
real    0m16.328s
user    0m0.039s
sys     0m0.100s
```

The main cause of these improvements is that we uploaded and downloaded the same images from our local network. We saved on the bandwidth of our Docker hosts, and our deployment time got shorter. The best part of all is that we no longer have to rely on the availability of Docker Hub in order to deploy.

 In order to deploy our Docker images to other Docker hosts, we need to set up security for our Docker registry. Details on how to set this up are outside the scope of this book; however, more details on how to set up a Docker registry are available at https://docs.docker.com/registry/ deploying.

Improving image build time

Docker images are the main artifacts that developers most of their time working on. The simplicity of Docker files and the speed of container technology allows us to enable rapid iteration on the application that we are working on; however, these advantages of using Docker start to diminish once the time it takes to build Docker images starts to grow uncontrollably. In this section, we will discuss some cases of building Docker images that take some time to run. We will then give you a few tips on how to remedy these effects by doing the following:

- Using registry mirrors
- Reusing image layers
- Reducing the build context size
- Using caching proxies

Using registry mirrors

A big contributor to image build time is the time spent fetching upstream images. Suppose we have a Dockerfile with the following line:

```
FROM openjdk:jre-stretch
```

This image will have to download `openjdk:jre-stretch` to be built. When we move to another Docker host, or if the `openjdk:jre-stretch` image is updated in Docker Hub, our build time will increase momentarily. Configuring a local registry mirror will reduce such increases in image build time.

This is very useful in an organization setting, where each developer has their own Docker hosts at their workstations. The organization's network only downloads the image from Docker Hub once. Each workstation Docker host in the organization can now directly fetch the images from the local registry mirror.

Setting up a registry mirror is as simple as the process of setting up a local registry in the previous section; however, in addition, we need to configure the Docker host to be aware of this registry mirror by passing the `--registry-mirror` option to the Docker daemon.

Go through the following steps to set this up:

1. In our CentOS Docker host, configure the Docker daemon by updating the configuration file, `/etc/docker/daemon.json`, as follows:

```
{
  "registry-mirrors": [
    "http://127.0.0.1:5000"
  ]
}
```

2. Next, restart the Docker daemon to start it with the newly configured `systemd` unit using the following command:

```
dockerhost$ systemctl restart docker.service
```

3. Finally, run the registry mirror Docker container using the following command:

```
dockerhost$ docker run --network=host -d \
    -e PROXY_REMOTEURL=https://registry-1.docker.io \
    registry:2
```

If we want to apply these changes to our cluster, we should update the base Chef recipe for our Docker Swarm nodes.

For the registry, it can be deployed as a proper service that is secure and managed by Docker Compose.

To confirm that the registry mirror works as expected, go through the following steps:

1. Build the Dockerfile described at the start of this subsection and take note of its build time. Note that most of the time needed to build the Docker image is taken up with downloading the upstream `openjdk:jre-stretch` Docker image, as shown in the following command:

```
dockerhost$ time docker build -t hubuser/mirror
Sending build context to Docker daemon  2.048kB
Step 1/1 : FROM openjdk:jre-stretch
jre-stretch: Pulling from library/openjdk
...
Status: Downloaded newer image for openjdk:jre-stretch
---> 9df4aac22102
Successfully built 9df4aac22102
Successfully tagged hubuser/mirror:latest
```

```
real      1m58.095s
user      0m0.036s
sys       0m0.028s
```

2. Now, remove the image and its upstream dependency and rebuild the image again using the following commands:

```
dockerhost$ docker rmi openjdk:jre-stretch hubuser/mirror
dockerhost$ time docker build -t hubuser/mirror
Sending build context to Docker daemon  2.048kB
Step 1/1 : FROM openjdk:jre-stretch
jre-stretch: Pulling from library/openjdk
...
Status: Downloaded newer image for openjdk:jre-stretch
---> 9df4aac22102
Successfully built 9df4aac22102
Successfully tagged hubuser/mirror:latest
real      0m24.422s
user      0m0.073s
sys       0m0.081
```

When the openjdk:jre-stretch Docker image was downloaded for the second time, it was retrieved from the local registry mirror instead of being connected to Docker Hub. Setting up a Docker registry mirror improved the time of downloading the upstream image by almost two times the usual. If we have other Docker hosts pointed at this same registry mirror, it will do the same thing: skip the process of downloading it from Docker Hub.

 This guide on how to set up a registry mirror is based on the one on the Docker documentation website. More details can be found at https://docs.docker.com/registry/recipes/mirror/.

Reusing image layers

As we already know, a Docker image consists of a series of layers combined with the union filesystem of a single image. When we work on building our Docker image, the preceding instructions in our Dockerfile are examined by Docker to check whether there is an existing image in its build cache that can be reused instead of creating a similar or duplicate image for these instructions.

By finding out how the build cache works, we can greatly increase the speed of the subsequent builds of our Docker images. A good example of this is when we develop our application's behavior; we will not add dependencies to our application all of the time. Most of the time, we will just want to update the core behavior of the application itself. Knowing this, we can design the way we will build our Docker images around this in our development workflow.

 Detailed rules on how `Dockerfile` instructions are cached can be found at `https://docs.docker.com/develop/develop-images/dockerfile_best-practices/#leverage-build-cache`.

For example, suppose we are working on a Ruby application whose source tree looks similar to the following:

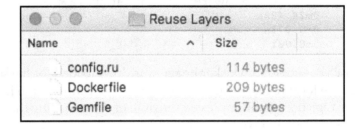

`config.ru` would be as follows:

```
app =  proc do |env|
  [200, {}, %w(hello world)]
end
run app
```

`Gemfile` would be as follows:

```
source 'https://rubygems.org'

gem 'rack'
gem 'nokogiri'
```

`Dockerfile` would be as follows:

```
FROM ruby:2.6.1

ADD . /app
WORKDIR /app
RUN bundle install

EXPOSE 9292
CMD rackup -E none
```

The following steps will show you how to build the Ruby application we wrote earlier as a Docker image:

1. First, let's build this Docker image using the following command. Note that the time it took to build is around one minute:

```
dockerhost$ time docker build -t slowdependencies .
Sending build context to Docker daemon 4.096kB
Step 1/6 : FROM ruby:2.6.1
. . .
Step 4/6 : RUN gem install -g
---> Running in 55ed0862f20a
Installing rack (2.0.6)
Installing mini_portile2 (2.4.0)
Installing nokogiri (1.10.1)
Building native extensions. This could take a while...
Removing intermediate container 55ed0862f20a
---> 61a50ca8c9a6
. . .
Successfully built af27ef83d1a2
Successfully tagged slowdependencies:latest
real 0m55.799s
user 0m0.035s
sys  0m0.039s
```

2. Next, update `config.ru` to change the application's behavior, as follows:

```
app = proc do |env|
  [200, {}, %w(hello other world)]
end
run app
```

3. Let's now build the Docker image again and note the time it takes to finish the build. Run the following command:

```
$ time docker build -t  slowdependencies .
...
Step 4/6 : RUN gem install -g
---> Running in 02c2daf0bc40
Installing rack (2.0.6)
Installing mini_portile2 (2.4.0)
Installing nokogiri (1.10.1)
Building native extensions. This could take a while...
...
Successfully tagged slowdependencies:latest
real      0m56.138s
user      0m0.028s
sys       0m0.051s
```

Note that, even with a single-line change to our application, we have to run `gem install -g` for each iteration of the Docker image that we are building. This can be very inefficient, and it disrupts the flow of our development because it takes one minute to build and run our Docker application. For impatient developers, this feels like an eternity!

In order to optimize this workflow, we can separate the phase in which we prepare our application's dependencies separately from our actual application. The next steps show us how to do this:

1. First, update our Dockerfile with the following changes:

```
FROM ruby:2.6.1

ADD Gemfile /app/Gemfile
WORKDIR /app
RUN gem install -g
ADD . /app

EXPOSE 9292
CMD rackup -E none
```

2. Next, build the newly refactored Docker image using this command:

```
dockerhost$ $ time docker build -t  fastdependencies .
Sending build context to Docker daemon  6.144kB
...
Step 4/7 : RUN gem install -g
---> Running in 01c6d0732716
Installing rack (2.0.6)
Installing mini_portile2 (2.4.0)
```

```
Installing nokogiri (1.10.1)
Building native extensions. This could take a while...
Removing intermediate container 01c6d0732716
---> 5d6848c306b6
...
Successfully tagged fastdependencies:latest
real     0m52.838s
user     0m0.034s
sys      0m0.039s
```

Let's take note of the intermediate container image ID generated by Step 4/7: gem install -g.

3. Now, let's update config.ru again and rebuild the image, as follows:

```
dockerhost$ vi config.ru # edit as we please
dockerhost$$ time docker build -t  fastdependencies .
...
...
Step 4/7 : RUN gem install -g
---> Using cache
---> 5d6848c306b6
Step 5/7 : ADD . /app
---> d917b622038b
...
Successfully tagged fastdependencies:latest
real     0m0.540s
user     0m0.036s
sys      0m0.046s
```

As we can see in the preceding output, docker build reused the cache until Step 4/7, as there was no change in Gemfile. Note that our Docker images build time decreased by 80 times the usual build time!

This kind of refactoring for our Docker image is also useful to reduce deployment time. Our Docker hosts in production already have image layers until Step 4/7 of our Docker image in the previous version of our container. A new version of our Docker application will only require the Docker host to pull new image layers from Step 4/7 to Step 7/7 in order to update our application.

Reducing the build context size

Let's suppose that we have a Dockerfile in the Git version control similar to the following:

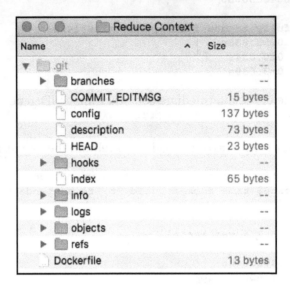

At some point, we will notice that our `.git` directory is too big. This is probably the result of having more and more code committed into our source tree:

```
dockerhost$ du -hsc .git
1001M   .git
1001M   total
```

Now, when we build our Docker application, we will notice that the amount of time taken to build our Docker application is very high as well. Take a look at the following output:

```
dockerhost$ time docker build -t hubuser/largecontext .
Sending build context to Docker daemon  1.024GB
...
Successfully tagged hubuser/largecontext:latest

real    0m12.638s
user    0m0.572s
sys     0m1.388s
```

If we look closely at the preceding output, we will see that the Docker client uploaded the whole `.git` directory of 1 GB onto the Docker daemon because it is a part of our build context. Also, as this is a large build context, it takes time for the Docker daemon to receive it before being able to start building our Docker image.

However, these files are not necessary to build our application. Moreover, these Git-related files are not at all needed when we run our application in production. We can set Docker to ignore a specific set of files that are not needed to build our Docker image. Follow the next few steps to perform this optimization:

1. Create a `.dockerignore` file with the following content in the same directory as our `Dockerfile`:

   ```
   .git
   ```

2. Finally, build our Docker image again by executing the following command:

   ```
   dockerhost$ time docker build -t hubuser/largecontext .
   Sending build context to Docker daemon   3.072kB
   ...
   Successfully tagged hubuser/largecontext:latest
   real    0m0.224s
   user    0m0.027s
   sys     0m0.070s
   ```

We can see in the output above that build time is reduced by over 500 times just by decreasing the size of the Docker's build context.

More information on how to use the `.dockerignore` files can be found at `https://docs.docker.com/reference/builder/#dockerignore-file`.

Using caching proxies

Another common problem that causes long runtimes in building Docker images is instructions that download dependencies. For example, a CentOS-based Docker image needs to fetch packages from YUM repositories. Depending on how large these packages are, the build time for a `yum install` instruction may be long.

A useful technique to reduce the time for these build instructions is to introduce proxies that cache such dependency packages. A popular caching proxy is `apt-cacher-ng`. This section will describe how to run and set it up to improve our Docker image building workflow.

The following is an example of `Dockerfile` that installs a lot of Debian packages:

```
FROM centos:7

RUN yum install -y java-11-openjdk-headless
```

Note that its build time in the following output is quite long because this `Dockerfile` file downloads a lot of dependencies and packages related to Java (`java-11-openjdk-headless`). Run the following command:

```
dockerhost$ time docker build -t beforecaching .
...
Successfully tagged beforecaching:latest

real    3m41.779s
user    0m0.035s
sys     0m0.079s
```

In order to improve the workflow for building this Docker image, we will set up a caching proxy with `apt-cacher-ng`. There are a few ready-to-run Docker images of `apt-cacher-ng` from Docker Hub. Follow the next few steps to prepare `apt-cacher-ng`:

> In general, it is recommended that we verify the contents of Docker images in environments, such as Docker Hub, instead of blindly trusting them.
>
> The page for the `apt-cacher-ng` Docker image we are using is found at `https://hub.docker.com/r/sameersbn/apt-cacher-ng`.

1. Run the following command in our Docker host to start `apt-cacher-ng`:

    ```
    dockerhost$ docker run -d --network=host sameersbn/apt-cacher-ng
    ```

2. We will create a new base Docker image. After this, we will use the caching proxy we ran earlier, as described in the following Dockerfile:

    ```
    FROM centos:7

    ADD proxy.conf /etc/yum/proxy.conf

    RUN sed -i 's/^mirr/#mirr/' /etc/yum.repos.d/CentOS-Base.repo && \
        sed -i 's/^#bas/bas/' /etc/yum.repos.d/CentOS-Base.repo
    ```

3. For the `proxy.conf` file inside our Docker image, we have the following entry so that YUM will download through our `apt-cacher-ng` installation:

   ```
   [main]
   proxy=http://dockerhost:3142
   ```

4. Build the `Dockerfile` we created earlier as a Docker image tagged as `hubuser/centos:7` using the following command line:

   ```
   dockerhost$ docker build -t hubuser/centos:7
   ```

5. Then, make `hubuser/debian:jessie` our new base Docker image by updating our `Dockerfile` that installs a lot of Debian packages for dependencies, such as the following:

   ```
   FROM hubuser/centos:7

   RUN yum install -y java-11-openjdk-headless
   ```

6. To confirm the new workflow, run an initial build to warm up the cache using the following command:

   ```
   dockerhost$ docker build -t aftercaching .
   ```

7. Finally, let's execute the following commands to build the image again. Make sure that you remove the image first:

   ```
   dockerhost$ docker rmi aftercaching dockerhost$ time docker build -t aftercaching .
   ...
   Successfully tagged aftercaching:latest
   real 0m33.942s
   user 0m0.039s
   sys  0m0.035s
   ```

Note how the subsequent build is faster, even though we do not use Docker's build cache. This technique is useful when we develop base Docker images for our team or organization. Team members that try to rebuild our Docker image will run their builds 6.5 times faster because they can download packages from our organization's cache proxy that we prepared earlier. Builds on our continuous integration server will also be faster upon check-in because we already warmed up the caching server during development.

In this section, we discussed how to use a very specific caching server. Here are a few others that we can use, along with their corresponding pages of documentation:

- **apt-cacher-ng**: This supports caching Debian, RPM, and other distribution-specific packages, and can be found at `https://www.unix-ag.uni-kl.de/~bloch/acng`.
- **Sonatype Nexus**: This supports Maven, Ruby Gems, PyPI, and NuGet packages out of the box. It is available at `http://www.sonatype.org/nexus`.
- **Polipo**: This is a generic caching proxy that is useful for development, and it can be found at `http://www.pps.univ-paris-diderot.fr/~jch/software/polipo`.
- **Squid**: This is another popular caching proxy that can work with other types of network traffic as well. You can look this up at `http://www.squid-cache.org`.

In the next section, we will examine some further details of how Docker's image layers work and how they affect the size of the resulting image. We will then learn how to optimize these image layers by exploiting how Docker images work.

Reducing Docker image size

As we keep working on our Docker applications, the sizes of the images will tend to get bigger and bigger if we are not careful. Most people using Docker observe that their team's custom Docker images increase in size to at least 1 GB or more. Having larger images means that the time to build and deploy our Docker application will increase as well. As a result, the feedback we get to determine the result of the application we're deploying gets reduced. This diminishes the benefits of Docker, enabling us to develop and deploy our applications in rapid iterations.

Chaining commands

Docker images grow big because some instructions are added that are unnecessary to build or run an image. Packaging metadata and cache are the common parts of the code that are usually increased in size. After installing the packages necessary to build and run our application, such downloaded packages are no longer needed. The following patterns of instructions in a Dockerfile are commonly found in the wild (such as in Docker Hub) to clean the images of such unnecessary files from Docker images:

```
FROM debian:stretch

RUN echo deb http://httpredir.debian.org/debian stretch-backports main \
    > /etc/apt/sources.list.d/stretch-backports.list
```

```
RUN apt-get update
RUN apt-get --no-install-recommends install -y openjdk-11-jre-headless
RUN rm -rfv /var/lib/apt/lists/*
```

However, a Docker image's size is basically the sum of each individual layer image; this is how union filesystems work. This means that the clean steps do not really delete the space. Take a look at the following commands:

```
dockerhost$ docker build -t fakeclean .
dockerhost$ docker history fakeclean
IMAGE           CREATED          CREATED BY                              SIZE
2fb3cfa78a67    3 minutes ago    /bin/sh -c rm -rfv /var/lib/apt/l... 0B
5c914734e883    3 minutes ago    /bin/sh -c apt-get --no-install-r... 220MB
f3d93082de54    4 minutes ago    /bin/sh -c apt-get update               17.5MB
de762158876a    4 minutes ago    /bin/sh -c echo deb http://httpre... 62B
d508d16c64cd    7 days ago       /bin/sh -c #(nop)  CMD ["bash"]         0B
<missing>       7 days ago       /bin/sh -c #(nop) ADD file:4fec87... 101MB
```

There is no such thing as negative layer size, and so each instruction in a Dockerfile can only keep the image size constant or increase it. Also, as each step introduces some metadata, the total size keeps increasing.

In order to reduce the total image size, the cleaning steps should be performed in the same image layer, and so the solution is to chain commands from multiple instructions into a single one. As Docker uses /bin/sh to run each instruction, we can use the Bourne shell's && operator to perform the chaining, as follows:

```
FROM debian:stretch

RUN echo deb http://httpredir.debian.org/debian stretch-backports main \
    > /etc/apt/sources.list.d/stretch-backports.list && \
    apt-get update && \
    apt-get --no-install-recommends install -y openjdk-11-jre-headless && \
    rm -rfv /var/lib/apt/lists/*
```

Note how each individual layer is much smaller now. As the individual layers' sizes were reduced, the total image size also decreased. Now, run the following commands and take a look at the output:

```
dockerhost$ docker build -t trueclean .
dockerhost$ docker history trueclean
IMAGE           CREATED          CREATED BY                              SIZE
d16c1aa0553a    3 minutes ago    /bin/sh -c echo deb http://httpredir... 220MB
d508d16c64cd    7 days ago       /bin/sh -c #(nop)  CMD ["bash"]         0B
<missing>       7 days ago       /bin/sh -c #(nop) ADD file:4fec879fd... 101MB
```

Separating build and deployment images

Another source of unnecessary files in Docker images is build time dependencies. Source libraries, such as compilers and source header files, are only necessary when building an application inside a Docker image. Once the application is built, these files are no longer necessary, as only the compiled binary and related shared libraries are needed to run the application.

To see an example of this, let's build the following application that is now ready to be deployed to a Docker host that we prepared in the cloud. The following source tree is a simple web application written in Go:

```
$ tree
.
├──── Dockerfile
├──── README.md
└──── hello.go

0 directories, 3 files
```

The following is the content of `hello.go` describing the application:

```
package main

import (
    "fmt"
    "net/http"
)

func handler(w http.ResponseWriter, r *http.Request) {
    fmt.Fprintf(w, "hello world")
}

func main() {
    http.HandleFunc("/", handler)
    http.ListenAndServe(":8080", nil)
}
```

The following corresponding Dockerfile shows how to build the source code and run the resulting binary:

```
FROM golang:1.11-stretch

ADD hello.go hello.go
RUN go build hello.go
```

```
EXPOSE 8080
ENTRYPOINT ["./hello"]
```

In the next few steps, we will show you how this Docker application's image size gets big:

1. First, let's build the Docker image:

   ```
   dockerhost $ docker build -t largeapp .
   ```

2. Next, let us take note of its size (823 MB), as shown in the following code:

   ```
   dockerhost$ docker build -t largeapp .
   dockerhost$ docker images
   REPOSITORY      TAG             IMAGE ID        CREATED         SIZE
   largeapp        latest          a10f9baee2e5    9 seconds ago   823MB
   golang          1.11-stretch    901414995ecd    6 days ago      816MB
   ```

3. To gather data for the next step, let's now run our application using the following:

   ```
   dockerhost$ docker run --name large -d largeapp
   ```

4. Let's enter the running container now to identify the actual size of our application, as shown in the following code:

   ```
   dockerhost$ docker exec -it large /bin/sh
   # ls -lh
   total 6.3M
   drwxrwxrwx. 2 root root      6 Feb  6 12:53 bin
   -rwxr-xr-x. 1 root root 6.3M Feb 13 11:09 hello
   -rw-r--r--. 1 root root  221 Feb 13 11:06 hello.go
   drwxrwxrwx. 2 root root      6 Feb  6 12:53 src
   ```

One of the advantages of writing Go applications, and compiled code in general, is that we can produce a single binary that is easy to deploy. The remaining size of the Docker image is made up of the unnecessary files provided by the base Docker image, such as the operating system and the Go compiler itself. In the steps we ran previously, the overhead coming from the base Docker image creates a total image size that is 100 times the original size!

We can optimize the end Docker image deployed to production by only packing the final hello binary and its shared libraries. Follow the next few steps to perform the optimization:

1. First, let's enter the container running our application again:

   ```
   dockerhost$ docker exec -it large /bin/sh
   ```

2. If the `hello` binary was compiled as a static library, we would now be done and could proceed with the next step. However, Go tooling builds shared binaries by default. In order for the binary to run properly, it needs the shared libraries. Let's run the following command inside our container to list these dependencies:

```
# ldd hello
linux-vdso.so.1 (0x00007ffce3fda000)
libpthread.so.0 => /lib/x86_64-linux-gnu/libpthread.so.0
(0x00007ff980d1c000)
libc.so.6 => /lib/x86_64-linux-gnu/libc.so.6 (0x00007ff98097d000)
/lib64/ld-linux-x86-64.so.2 (0x00007ff980f39000)
```

3. With this knowledge, we can now update our Dockerfile to utilize a multi-stage build process. We will copy our binary and its library dependencies to the next build stage:

```
FROM golang:1.11-stretch

ADD hello.go hello.go
RUN go build hello.go

# Good to have a base image that has some debugging tools
FROM busybox

COPY --from=0 /go/hello /app/hello
COPY --from=0 /lib/x86_64-linux-gnu/libpthread.so.0 \
                /lib/x86_64-linux-gnu/libpthread.so.0
COPY --from=0 /lib/x86_64-linux-gnu/libc.so.6 /lib/x86_64-linux-
gnu/libc.so.6
COPY --from=0 /lib64/ld-linux-x86-64.so.2 /lib64/ld-linux-
x86-64.so.2
WORKDIR /app
EXPOSE 8080
ENTRYPOINT ["./hello"]
```

4. Let's now rebuild our Docker image. As we can see from the following output, the resulting image size is much smaller:

```
dockerhost$ docker images
REPOSITORY     TAG             IMAGE ID        CREATED          SIZE
binary-only    latest          5c33cc2b31cd    4 minutes ago    9.74MB
largeapp       latest          a10f9baee2e5    21 minutes ago   823MB
golang         1.11-stretch    901414995ecd    6 days ago       816MB
busybox        latest          3a093384ac30    6 weeks ago      1.2MB
```

The same approach can also be used to make other compiled applications, such as the software normally installed using the `./configure && make && make install` combinations. We can do the same for interpreted languages, such as Python, Ruby, or PHP; however, it will need a little more work to create a runtime Ruby Docker image from a build Ruby Docker image. A good time to start investigating this kind of optimization is when the delivery of our applications gets too long because the images are too big for a sustainable development workflow.

Guide to Optimization

The techniques specified in this chapter are not comprehensive; more ways to achieve these objectives will surely be found as more people discover how to use Docker for their applications. More techniques will also arise as Docker itself matures and develops more features. The most important guiding factor for these optimizations is to ask ourselves whether we are really getting the benefits of using Docker. Some good example questions to ask are as follows:

- Is deploy time improving?
- Is the development team getting feedback fast enough from the operations team based on what the operations team learned when running our application?
- Are we able to iterate on new features fast enough to incorporate the new feedback that we discovered from customers using our application?

By keeping in mind our motivation and objective for using Docker, we can come up with our own ways to improve our workflows.

Summary

In this chapter, you learned more about how Docker builds images and applied that knowledge to improve several factors, such as the deploy time, build time, and image size. We also learned a few points to guide us further in our optimization journey.

In the next chapter, we will take these optimized Docker images we built and deploy them.

Deploying Containers 5

In this chapter, we will use Jenkins, running in a Docker container, to trigger a build of an application, push it to Docker Hub, and then deploy it in our Docker Swarm cluster.

In this chapter, we will cover the following topics:

- Building a custom Jenkins image
- Deploying Jenkins in our Docker Swarm cluster
- Configuring Jenkins to interact with our Docker Swarm cluster and Docker Hub account
- Building and deploying a simple application using a three-stage pipeline

Deploying and configuring Jenkins

Jenkins originally started life as an open source build server, originally called **Hudson** (the name was changed following a dispute with Oracle), whose sole purpose was to compile Java applications. Since it was first released in 2004, its role has been greatly expanded and it is now considered to be one of the leading continuous integration and continuous delivery solutions available and not just a build server for Java applications.

Before we can deploy our test application, we need to deploy and configure Jenkins. The following are the steps you need to take to get a full Jenkins server deployed and configured.

Deploying the Jenkins container

Before we launch and configure our Jenkins container in our Docker Swarm cluster, we need to create an image. For this, we will be using the official Jenkins image as a base and then we will add a few of our own customizations:

1. We will start by preparing a Jenkins configuration file; the file should be named `init.groovy.d/plugins.groovy`. This file will be loaded when the container first starts and will instruct Jenkins to install a few of the prerequisites we require. The contents of the file should be as follows:

```groovy
import jenkins.model.Jenkins;

pm = Jenkins.instance.pluginManager
uc = Jenkins.instance.updateCenter
uc.updateAllSites()

installed = false

["git", "workflow-aggregator"].each {
  if (! pm.getPlugin(it)) {
    deployment = uc.getPlugin(it).deploy(true)
    deployment.get()
    installed = true
  }
}

if (installed) {
  Jenkins.instance.restart()
}
```

2. Now that we have our `init.groovy.d/plugins.groovy` file, we can move on to our actual Docker image. Then, place the following content into a file called `Dockerfile`. As you can see, we are using the long-term support version of the Jenkins image, which can be found at `https://hub.docker.com/r/jenkins/jenkins`.

   Another interesting thing to note is that we are also installing Docker itself within the image; we are doing this so that Jenkins has a way of interacting with our Docker Swarm cluster. We will look at configuring this later in the chapter:

```dockerfile
FROM jenkins/jenkins:lts

ARG docker_version=18.09.5
ARG
```

```
docker_tarball=https://download.docker.com/linux/static/stable/x86_
64/docker-$docker_version.tgz

LABEL com.docker.version=$docker_version

USER root
RUN cd /usr/local/bin && \
    curl -s $docker_tarball | tar xz docker/docker --strip-
components=1

USER jenkins
COPY init.groovy.d/plugins.groovy \
        /usr/share/jenkins/ref/init.groovy.d/plugins.groovy
```

3. Now that we have the basic configuration files in place, we can build our Jenkins Docker image and push it to Docker Hub using the following commands. Remember to make sure that you replace hubuser with your own Docker Hub username:

```
$ docker build -t hubuser/jenkins:latest .
$ docker push hubuser/jenkins:latest
```

4. Before we launch our Jenkins containers, we need to prepare a service definition in a compose file. Create a file called docker-compose.yml and enter the following, again making sure that you update hubuser to be that of your own Docker Hub username:

```
version: '3.7'

services:
  jenkins:
    image: hubuser/jenkins:latest
    ports:
      - '8080:8080'
    deploy:
      replicas: 1
```

5. We should be able to deploy Jenkins using the service definition we have just created by running the following code:

```
$ docker stack deploy jenkins --compose-file docker-compose.yml
```

As we have instructed Jenkins to do an initial configure using the init.groovy.d/plugins.groovy file when it first starts, it may take a few moments to launch and download the additional plugins; you can check the status of the stack by running the following code:

```
$ docker stack ls
$ docker stack services jenkins
```

Once you see the 1/1 replicas, your Jenkins container should be ready and we can move on to completing the installation in our browser.

Finishing the Jenkins Configuration

When opening your browser and going to http://dockerhost:8080, ensuring that you replace dockerhost with the IP address of your Docker Swarm host, you should be greeted with a page that looks like the following:

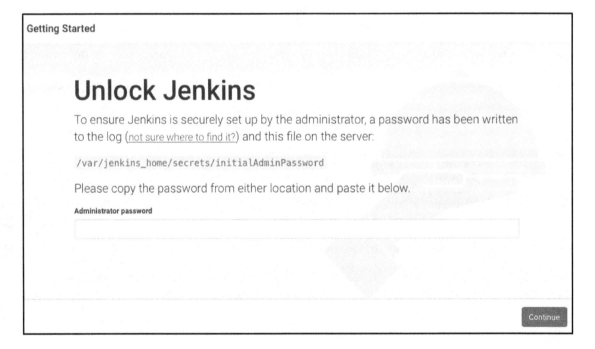

As you can see, one of the things that Jenkins does when it first starts is to secure itself—with good reason too; if your Jenkins instance was publicly available, then you would not want it exposed with a default username and password configured, as there are bots that were built to target and compromise Jenkins installation, that are waiting to be configured.

To find the administrator password, which is a 32-character alpha-numeric string, we simply need to run the following two commands:

```
$ container=jenkins_jenkins.1.$(docker service ps jenkins_jenkins -q)
$ docker exec $container cat /var/jenkins_home/secrets/initialAdminPassword
```

The first command generates the full container name and the second command uses the `docker exec` command to print out the contents of the `/var/jenkins_home/secrets/initialAdminPassword` file to the screen, or, in our case, output the password.

Entering the administrator password in the space provided and clicking on the **Continue** button will take you to a page that gives you two choices:

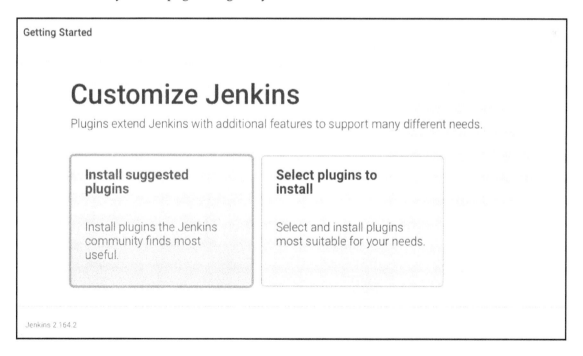

From here, select the second choice, **Select plugins to install**. On the page that is then loaded, you have several options to choose from; however, as we have installed the plugins we need when Jenkins first started, you will be able to click on **None**, which can be found in the top menu and deselects everything, then click on the **Install** button:

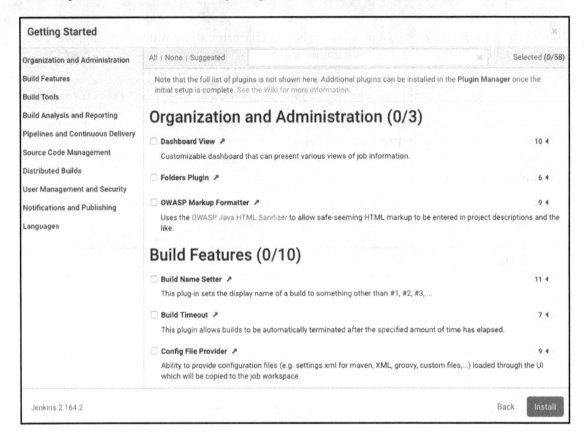

As there is nothing to install, this will take you to a page where you can create your own admin user. Here, you can enter your preferred username/password combination or you can continue to use the admin username and password that was generated when Jenkins first launched:

Getting Started

Create First Admin User

Username:

Password:

Confirm password:

Full name:

E-mail address:

Jenkins 2.164.2   Continue as admin   Save and Continue

The final step of the configuration is to confirm the Jenkins URL. This is pre-populated with the URL you are currently accessing Jenkins on; for most people, this will be fine and you can click on the **Save and Finish** button to complete the configuration:

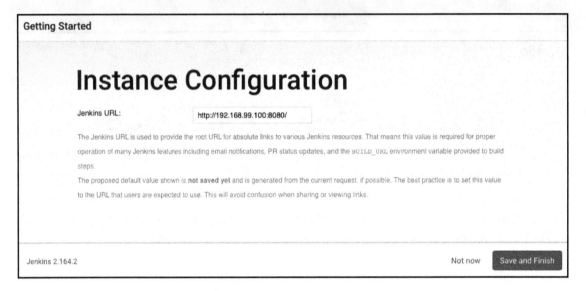

That should complete the setup, and, as per the message on the screen shown in the following screenshot, you are able to start using Jenkins:

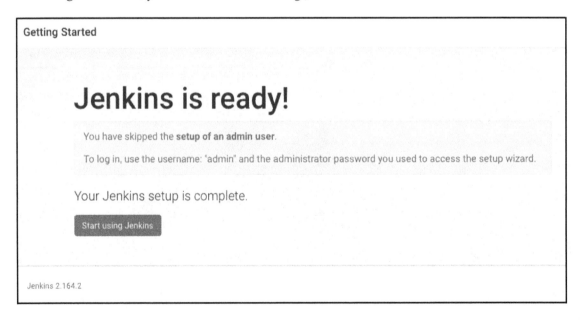

Now you have a working Jenkins installation, we can start to tell it about our Docker Swarm cluster.

Setting up our Docker credentials within Jenkins

There are a few different steps to providing access to our Swarm cluster, as well as our Docker Hub account, so that our recently deployed Jenkins container can build, push, and deploy containers for us.

Let's start by providing the certificates required to access our Docker Swarm cluster. You can enter these credentials by going to `http://dockerhost:8080/credentials/store/system/domain/_/newCredentials` (don't forget to update the URL as needed) or by clicking on **Credentials** > **System** > **Global credentials (unrestricted)** and then clicking on **Add Credentials**.

On the form you are presented with, set **Kind** to `Docker Host Certificate Authentication` and the form should change, asking for the following details:

1. **Client Key**: Paste the contents of the `~/.docker/key.pem` file on your Docker host
2. **Client Certificate**: Paste the contents from the `~/.docker/cert.pem` file on your Docker host
3. **Server CA Certificate**: Paste the contents from the `~/.docker/ca.pem` file on your Docker host
4. **ID**: Enter `docker-swarm`
5. Click on **OK**

This should look something like the following:

Remember the reference to this secret `docker-swarm` credentials as we will be using this later. Next, we need to provide Jenkins with our Docker Hub credentials. To do this, click on **Add Credentials** again. This time, leave the **Kind** at **Username** with **Password**, which should be the default option:

1. **Username**: Enter your Docker Hub username, for example, `hubuser`
2. **Password**: Enter your Docker Hub password
3. **Id**: Use `dockerhub`—we will refer to this later

Now that we have the credentials added to our Jenkins installation, we are ready to look at creating a Jenkins pipeline, which will utilize these credentials and build a test application.

Building and deploying a container

Now that Jenkins has been configured, we need to decide on an application to configure and deploy.

Preparing our application

If you recall, in Chapter 4, *Optimizing Docker Images*, we created a simple Go application, which prints hello world to the screen when you open it in a browser. Dockerfile contained a multi-stage build that looked like the following:

```
FROM golang:1.11-stretch

ADD hello.go hello.go
RUN go build hello.go

FROM busybox
COPY --from=0 /go/hello /app/hello
COPY --from=0 /lib/x86_64-linux-gnu/libpthread.so.0 \
             /lib/x86_64-linux-gnu/libpthread.so.0
COPY --from=0 /lib/x86_64-linux-gnu/libc.so.6 /lib/x86_64-linux-
gnu/libc.so.6
COPY --from=0 /lib64/ld-linux-x86-64.so.2 /lib64/ld-linux-x86-64.so.2
WORKDIR /app
EXPOSE 8080
ENTRYPOINT ["./hello"]
```

The hello.go file contains the following:

```
package main

import (
  "fmt"
  "net/http"
)

func handler(w http.ResponseWriter, r *http.Request) {
  fmt.Fprintf(w, "hello world")
}

func main() {
  http.HandleFunc("/", handler)
  http.ListenAndServe(":8080", nil)
}
```

In addition to the preceding two files, we need to add Jenkinsfile. As you have probably guessed by the filename, this is similar to a Dockerfile in that it defines how Jenkins should build our application. The Jenkinsfile for our application is separated into three build stages:

1. **Build Docker image**: This stage builds the image locally using the Dockerfile from our application
2. **Publish to Docker Hub**: This stage takes the image built by the first stage and pushes it to Docker Hub
3. **Deploy to production**: This final stage deploys our application using the image that was pushed to Docker Hub:

```
node {
    def app
    stage('Build Docker Image') {
        checkout scm
        docker.withServer('tcp://dockerhost:2376', 'docker-swarm')
{
            app = docker.build('hubuser/jenkins-app:latest')
        }
    }
    stage('Publish to Docker Hub') {
        docker.withServer('tcp://dockerhost:2376', 'docker-swarm')
{
            docker.withRegistry("https://index.docker.io/v1/",
"dockerhub") {
                app.push('latest')
            }
        }
    }

    stage('Deploy to Production') {
        docker.withServer('tcp://dockerhost:2376', 'docker-swarm')
{
            sh "docker service update app --force --image
${app.id}"
        }
    }
}
```

We will be using Git to distribute the configuration for our application. This is made up of the following three files, `Dockerfile`, `hello.go`, and `Jenkinsfile`. I would recommend cloning the example repository, which can be found on GitHub at `https://github.com/dockerhp/jenkins-app` and is publicly available.

As you can see, the two sets of credentials are being referenced within `Jenkinsfile`, where we need to interact with our Docker Swarm cluster. The `docker-swarm` credentials are referenced, and, for where we need to log in to the Docker Hub, we are referencing `dockerhub`. This means that, while your `Jenkinsfile` is publicly available, you are never actually exposing any sensitive information, such as the certificates or your Docker Hub logins in the repository—everything is stored safely within your Jenkins installation.

Before we progress, you will need to edit the `Jenkinsfile` and make sure that all references of `tcp://dockerhost:2376` are updated to reflect the IP/hostname of your Docker host and that `hubuser` is updated to reflect your own Docker Hub user. Finally, make sure that your `Jenkinsfile` is committed and pushed to your Git repository.

Once updated, we can deploy the service, which will eventually host our application by running the following:

```
$ docker service create --name app --publish 80:8080 nginx
```

As you may have noticed, we are deploying the official NGINX image and not our application; don't worry, the third stage of the build replaces this with the correct image. You can quickly test the deployment by running the following command:

```
$ curl http://dockerhost
curl: (7) Failed connect to dockerhost:80; Connection refused
```

As you can see, it failed! However, that is to be expected, as we haven't really configured NGINX correctly. In the next section, we will create a Jenkins job, which will use the pipeline defined in our `Jenkinsfile` to finally deploy our application.

Creating a Jenkins job

We have reached the final part of our deployment. Here, we will pull all of the bits we have so far configured together into a build pipeline that will build and deploy our application. To start with, we need to create a new job; you can do this by going to `http://dockerhost:8080/newJob`. Here, you will be presented with five different types of Jenkins jobs:

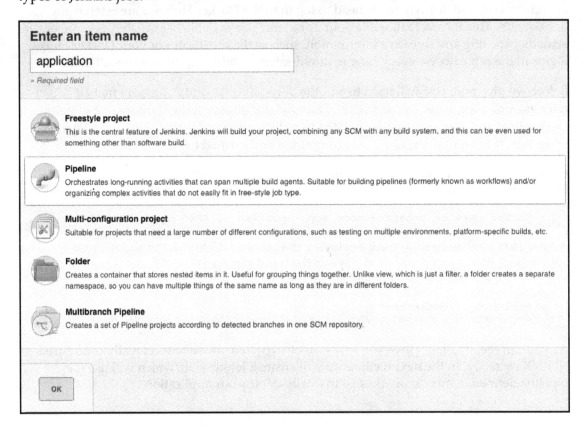

On this page, **Enter an item name** of `application`, select **Pipeline**, and click on **OK**.

On the page that loads, there are several options, scroll down past **General**, **Build Triggers**, and **Advanced Project Options** down to **Pipeline**.

By default, the definition will have **Pipeline script** selected. As our pipeline is being defined in a `Jenkinsfile` hosted in our Git repository, update the definition to **Pipeline script from SCM.** This will update the form with the dropdown next to **SCM** reading **None.** Update this so that **Git** is selected.

In the **Repository URL** box, enter the HTTPS URL for your Git repository, for example, `https://github.com/dockerhp/jenkins-app.git`. Leave all other fields to their default and click on **Save**.

This should take you to a page that looks like the following:

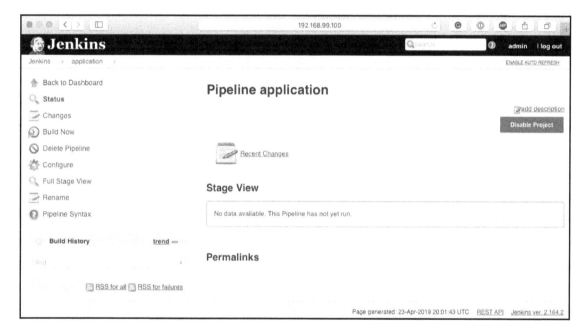

All that is left to do is to click on **Build Now**.

Running the Pipeline

When you click **Build Now,** you should see a job appear at the bottom of the left-hand side menu, click on the job number and then **Console Output** will give you a real-time view of the job being executed and you should see something similar to the following:

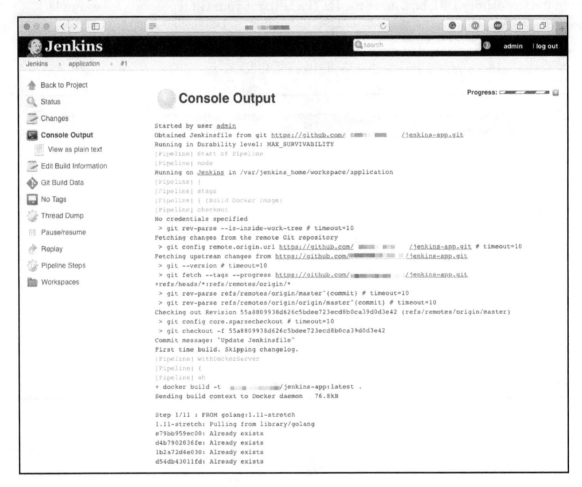

Once completed, returning to the application in Jenkins should show you something like the following page:

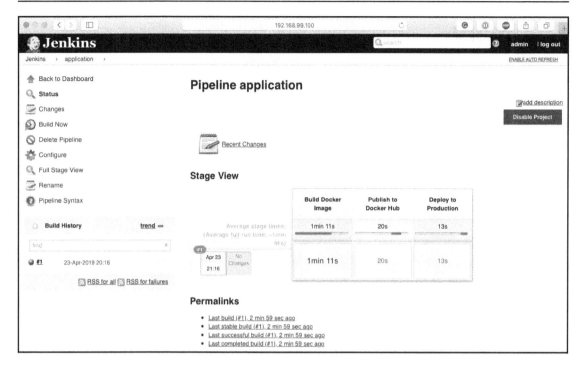

As you can see, our three build stages all completed successfully. If, for any reason, your build failed, you should be able to review the **Console Output.** I would recommend that you correctly update the Docker URL and Docker Hub username in the Jenkins file—if you need to rerun the build, make sure your changes are committed, push them to GitHub, and then click on **Build Now** again.

Once deployed, running the following command should return `hello world`:

```
$ curl http://dockerhost
hello world
```

While this is a really basic example, it is hard to see how this can approach could be advantageous; for example, without much more effort, you could configure a webhook in Jenkins to watch your GitHub repository and, every time a change is detected, your pipeline can be automatically triggered to build, publish, and deploy your updated container.

Summary

In this chapter, we have looked at how we can use Jenkins to build, distribute, and deploy our containerized application. For more information on Jenkins, see the project's website at `https://jenkins.io/`.

In the next chapter, we will start doing performance tests and benchmark how our deployed Docker applications fare under load.

6
Benchmarking

In optimizing our Docker applications, it is important to validate the parameters that we tuned. Benchmarking is an experimental way of identifying whether the elements we modified in our Docker containers performed as expected. Our application will have a wide area of options to be optimized. The Docker hosts running them have their own set of parameters, such as memory, networking, CPU, and storage, as well. Depending on the nature of our application, one or more of these parameters can become a bottleneck. Having a series of tests to validate each component with benchmarks is important for guiding our optimization strategy.

Additionally, by creating proper performance tests, we can identify the limits of the current configuration of our Docker-based application. With this information, we can start exploring infrastructure parameters, such as scaling out our application by deploying them on more Docker hosts. We can also use this information to scale up the same application by moving our workload to a Docker host with higher storage, memory, or CPU, and when we have hybrid cloud deployments, we can use these measurements to identify which cloud provider gives our application its optimum performance.

Measuring how our application responds to these benchmarks is important when planning the capacity needed for our Docker infrastructure. By creating a test workload simulating peak and normal conditions, we can predict how our application will perform once it is released to production. Note that we can easily apply learnings we got from our benchmarks because we have a reliable and consistent way of deploying containers from Chapter 5, *Deploying Containers*.

In this chapter, we will cover the following topics to benchmark a simple web application deployed in our Docker infrastructure:

- Setting up Apache JMeter for benchmarking
- Creating and designing a benchmark workload
- Analyzing application performance

Setting up Apache JMeter

Apache JMeter is a popular application that is used for testing the performance of web servers. Besides load testing web servers, the open source project grew to support testing other network protocols, such as LDAP, FTP, and even raw TCP packets. It is highly configurable, and powerful enough to design complex workloads of different usage patterns. This feature can be used to simulate thousands of users suddenly visiting our web application, thereby inducing a spike in the load.

Another feature expected in any load-testing software is its data capture and analysis functions. JMeter has such a wide variety of data recording, plotting, and analysis features that we can explore the results of our benchmarks right away. Finally, it has a wide variety of plugins that may already have the load pattern, analysis, or network connection that we plan to use.

 More information about the features and how to use Apache JMeter can be found on its website at `http://jmeter.apache.org`.

In this section, we will deploy an example application to benchmark and prepare our workstation to run our first JMeter-based benchmark.

Deploying a sample application

We can also bring our own web application that we want to benchmark if we please. But for the rest of this chapter, we will benchmark the following application described in this section. The application is a simple Ruby web application deployed using Unicorn, a popular Ruby application server. It receives traffic via a Unix socket from NGINX. This setup is very typical for most Ruby applications found in the wild.

In this section, we will deploy this Ruby application in a Docker host called `webapp`. We will use separate Docker hosts for the application, benchmark tools, and monitoring. This separation is important so that the benchmark and monitoring instrumentation we run don't affect the benchmark results.

The next few steps show us how to build and deploy our simple Ruby web application stack:

1. First, create the Ruby application by creating the following Rack `config.ru` file:

```
app =  proc do |env|
  Math.sqrt rand
  [200, {}, %w(hello world)]
end
run app
```

2. Next, we package the application as a Docker container with the following `Dockerfile`:

```
FROM ruby:2.6

RUN gem install --no-doc unicorn rack
WORKDIR /app

COPY config.ru /app/config.ru

CMD unicorn -l 8000
```

3. Build the application and push to Docker Hub using the following code:

```
$ docker build -t hubuser/benchmark-app .
$ docker push hubuser/benchmark-app
```

4. The last component will be a `compose.yml` file that will describe how our application will run inside our Docker Swarm cluster, as shown in the following code:

```
---
version: '3.7'

services:
  web:
    image: aespinosa/benchmark-app
    ports:
      - 8000:8000

# Set for debugging and testing purposes
networks:
  default:
    driver: overlay
    attachable: true
```

In the end, we will have the files shown in the following screenshot in our code base:

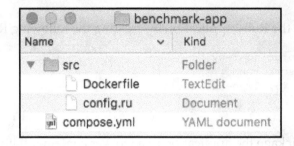

Now that we have our application ready, let's deploy and test our application by going through the following steps:

1. First, let's deploy our application by running the following command:

```
dockerhost$ docker stack deploy app -c compose.yml
```

2. Then, let's conduct a simple test to determine whether our application works properly:

```
$ curl http://dockerhost:8000
hello world
```

We are now done preparing the application that we want to benchmark. In the next section, we will prepare our workstation to perform the benchmarks by installing Apache JMeter.

Installing JMeter

For the rest of this chapter, we will use Apache JMeter version 5.1 to perform our benchmarks. In this section, we will download and install it in our workstation. Follow the next few steps to set up JMeter properly:

1. To begin, go to JMeter's download web page at http://jmeter.apache.org/download_jmeter.cgi.
2. Select the link for apache-jmeter-5.1.tgz to begin downloading the binary.

3. When the download finishes, extract the tarball by typing the following command:

```
$ tar -xzf apache-jmeter-5.1.tgz
```

4. Next, we will add the `bin/` directory to our `$PATH` variable so that JMeter can be easily launched from the command line. To do this, we will type the following command in our Terminal:

```
$ export PATH=$PATH:$(pwd)/apache-jmeter-5.1/bin
```

5. Finally, let's launch JMeter by typing the following command:

```
$ jmeter
```

We will now see the JMeter UI, as shown in the following screenshot:

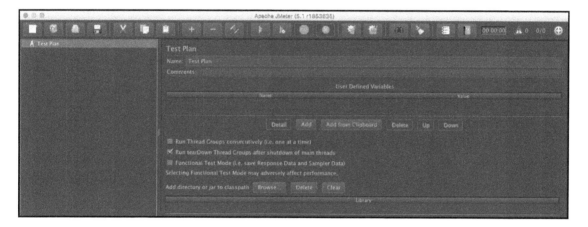

We are now ready to write the benchmark for our application!

Apache JMeter is a Java application. According to the JMeter website, it requires at least Java 8 to work. Make sure you have a **Java Runtime Environment (JRE)** properly set up before installing JMeter.

If we were in a macOS X environment, we could use Homebrew and just type the following command:

```
$ brew install jmeter
```

For other platforms, the instructions described earlier should be sufficient to get started. More information on how to install JMeter can be found at `http://jmeter.apache.org/usermanual/get-started.html`.

Building a benchmark workload

Writing benchmarks for an application is an open-ended area to explore. Apache JMeter can be overwhelming at first: it has several options to tune in order to write our benchmarks. To begin, we can use the story of our application as a start. The following are some of the questions we can ask ourselves:

- What does our application do?
- What is our users' demographic?
- How do they interact with our application?

Starting with the preceding questions, we can then translate them into actual requests that we can use to test our application.

In the sample application that we wrote, we have a web application that displays `Hello World` to our users. In web applications, we are typically interested with the throughput and response time. Throughput refers to the number of users that can receive `Hello World` at a time. Response time describes the time lag before the user receives the `Hello World` message from the moment they requested it.

In this section, we will create a preliminary benchmark in Apache JMeter. Then, we will begin analyzing our initial results with JMeter's analysis tools and the monitoring stack that we deployed in `Chapter 3`, *Monitoring Docker*. After that, we will iterate on the benchmarks we developed and tune it. This way, we will know that we are benchmarking our application properly.

Creating a test plan in JMeter

A series of benchmarks in Apache JMeter is described in a test plan. A test plan describes a series of steps that JMeter will execute, such as sending requests to a web application. Each step in a test plan is called an element. These elements themselves can have one or more elements as well. In the end, our test plan will look like a tree—a hierarchy of elements to describe the benchmark we want for our application.

To add an element into our test plan, we simply right-click on the parent element that we want and then select **Add**. This opens a context menu of elements that can be added to the selected parent element. In the following screenshot, we add a **Thread Group** element to the main element, **Test Plan**, as shown in the following screenshot:

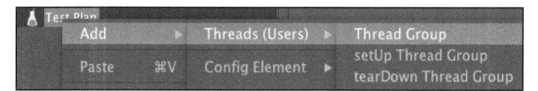

The next few steps show us the way to create a test plan conducting the benchmark that we want:

1. First, let's rename the test plan as something more appropriate. Click on the **Test Plan** element; this will update the main JMeter window on the right. In the form field labeled **Name**, set the value to **Unicorn Capacity**.

2. Under the **Unicorn Capacity** test plan, create a thread group. Name this `Application Users`. We will configure this thread group to send `10000` requests to our application from a single thread in the beginning. Use the following parameters to fill out the form to configure this setting:
    * **Number of Threads**: 1
    * **Ramp-up Period**: 0 seconds
    * **Loop Count**: `10000` times

When we start developing our test plans, having a low **Loop Count** is useful. Instead of `10000` loop counts, we can begin with 100 or even just 10 instead. Our benchmarks are shorter and we get immediate feedback when developing it, even as soon as the next step. When we finish the whole test plan, we can always revert and tune it later to generate more requests.

3. Next, under the `Application Users` thread group, we create the actual request by adding **Sampler, HTTP Request**. The following is the configuration where we set the details of how we make a request to our web application:
   - **Name**: Go to `http://dockerhost:8000/`
   - **Server Name**: `dockerhost`
   - **Port Number**: `8000`

4. In our test plan, we will now describe how to save the test results by adding a *listener* under the **Unicorn Capacity** test plan. For this, we will add a **Simple Data Writer** and name it **Save Result**. We set the **Filename** field to `result.jtl` to save our benchmark results in said file. We will refer to this file later when we analyze the result of the benchmark.

5. Finally, let's save the test plan we created by going to **File** then **Save**. For the filename, let's call our test plan `benchmark.jmx`.

Now, we have a basic benchmark workload that generates 10,000 HTTP requests to `http://dockerhost:8000/`. The following is a screenshot of JMeter when we created our test plan:

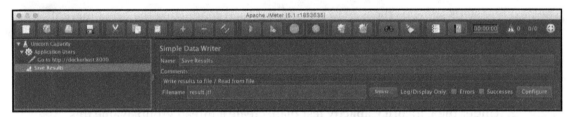

Finally, it is time to run our benchmark. Let's exit the JMeter UI and go back to our Terminal. We will type the following command to perform the actual benchmark:

```
$ jmeter -n -t benchmark.jmx
```

After running the benchmark, the test results were saved in a file called `result.jtl`, which we used when making this test plan earlier. We will examine these results by using JMeter's analysis tools in the next section.

There are various types of elements that can be placed in a JMeter test plan. Besides the three elements we used previously to create a basic benchmark for our application, there are several others that regulate requests, perform other network requests, and analyze data.

A comprehensive list of test plan elements and their descriptions can be found on the JMeter page at `http://jmeter.apache.org/usermanual/component_reference.html`.

Analyzing benchmark results

In this section, we will analyze the benchmark results and identify how the 120,000 requests affected our application. In creating web application benchmarks, there are typically two things we are usually interested in:

- How many requests can our application handle at a time?
- For how long is each request being processed by our application?

These two low-level web-performance metrics can easily translate to the business implications of our application. For example, how many customers are using our application? Another one is, how are they perceiving the responsiveness of our application from a user-experience perspective? We can correlate secondary metrics in our application such as CPU, memory, and network to determine our system capacity.

Viewing the results of JMeter runs

Several listener elements of JMeter have features that render graphs. Enabling this when running the benchmark is useful when developing the test plan. But the time taken by the UI to render the results in real time, in addition to the actual benchmark requests, affects the performance of the test, which is why it is better for us to separate the execution and analysis components of our benchmark. In this section, we will create a new test plan and look at a few JMeter listener elements to analyze the data we acquired in `result.jtl`.

To begin our analysis, we first create a new test plan and name this `Analyze Results`. We will add various listener elements under this test plan parent element. After this, follow the next few steps to add various JMeter listeners that can be used to analyze our benchmark result.

Calculating throughput

For our first analysis, we will use the **Summary Report** listener. This listener will show the throughput of our application. A measurement of throughput will show the number of transactions our application can handle per second. After loading the listener, fill out the **Filename** field by selecting the `result.jtl` file that we generated when we ran our benchmark. For the run we did earlier, the following screenshot shows that the **10100** HTTP requests were sent to `http://dockerhost:8000/` at a throughput of **7.1** requests per second:

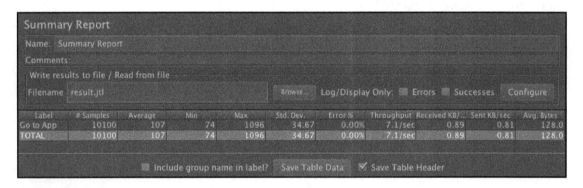

We can also look at how throughput evolved over the course of our benchmark with the **Graph Results** listener. Create this listener under the `Analyze Results` test plan element and name it `Throughput over time`. Make sure that only the **Throughput** checkbox is marked (feel free to look at the other data points later, though). After creating the listener, load our `result.jtl` test result again. The following screenshot shows how the throughput evolved over time:

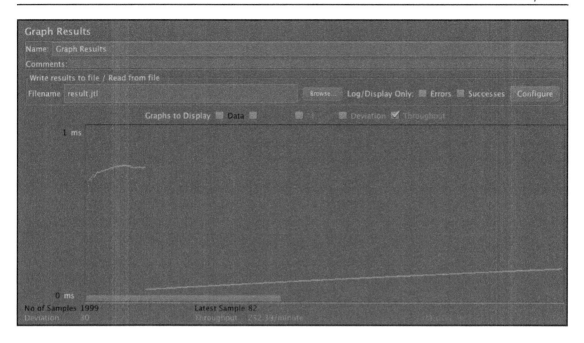

As we can see in the preceding screenshot, the throughput started slow while JMeter tried to warm up its single thread pool of requests. But after our benchmark continued to run, the throughput level settled at a stable level. By having a large number of loop counts earlier in our thread group, we were able to minimize the effect of the earlier **Ramp-up Period**.

This way, the throughput displayed in the **Summary Report** earlier is more or less a consistent result. Take note that the **Graph Results** listener wraps around its data points after several samples.

Remember that, in benchmarking, the more samples we get, the more precise our observations will be!

Plotting response time

Another metric we are interested in when we benchmark our application is the response time. The response time shows the time that JMeter has to wait before receiving the web page response from our application. In terms of real users, we can look at this as the time between when our users typed our web application's URL when everything was displayed in their web browser (this may not represent the real state of affairs if our application renders some slow JavaScript, but for the application we made earlier, this analogy should suffice).

To view the response time of our application, we will use the **Response Time Graph** listener. As an initial setting, we can set the interval to 500 milliseconds. This will average some of the response times along 500 milliseconds in the `result.jtl` file. In the following graph, you can see that our application's response time is mostly at around 1 millisecond:

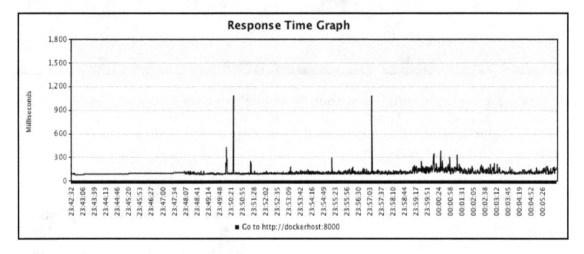

If we want to display the response time in finer detail, we can decrease the interval to as low as 1 millisecond. Take note that this will take more time to display as the JMeter UI tries to plot more points in the application. Sometimes, when there are too many samples, JMeter may crash because our workstation doesn't have enough memory to display the entire graph. In the case of large benchmarks, we are better off observing the results with our monitoring system. We will look at this data in the next section.

Observing performance in Grafana and Kibana

We might be faced with a situation where our workstation is so old that Java is not able to handle displaying 10,000 data points in its JMeter UI. To solve this, we can reduce the amount of data we have by either generating fewer requests in our benchmark or averaging out some of the data, like we did earlier when graphing the response time. However, sometimes we want to see the full resolution of our data. This full view is useful when we want to inspect the finer details of how our application behaves. Fortunately, we already have a monitoring system in place for our Docker infrastructure that we built in `Chapter 3`, *Monitoring Docker*.

Our Ruby application logs requests in its standard output stream in a format called the Apache **Common Log Format** (**CLF**). These events are captured by our Docker daemon and sent to the Logstash service we built in `Chapter 3`, *Monitoring Docker*. After the Logstash GELF collector receives the logs, it gets forwarded and stored in our Elasticsearch service. We can then use the visualize feature of Kibana to look at the throughput of our application. The following analysis was made by counting the number of access log entries that Elasticsearch received per second:

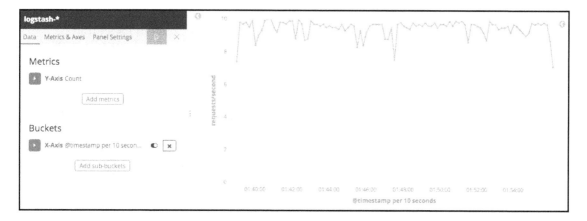

We can also plot our application's response time during the course of the benchmark in Kibana. To do this, we need to update our Logstash service with the following steps:

1. First, we need to update the `logstash.conf` file that configures our Logstash service. We will be adding the `grok {}` filter as follows:

```
# input { ... }
# output { ... }

filter {
  if [container_name] =~ /app_web/ {
    grok {
      match => {
        "message" => "%{HTTPD_COMMONLOG}\
%{NUMBER:response_time:float}"
      }
    }
  }
}
```

 Logstash's filter plugins are used to intermediately process events before they reach our target storage endpoint, such as Elasticsearch. It transforms raw data, such as lines of text, into a richer data schema in JSON that we can then use later for further analysis. More information about Logstash filter plugins can be found at `https://www.elastic.co/guide/en/logstash/current/filter-plugins.html`.

2. Next, we will redeploy our Logstash service. The following commands will recreate Logstash:

```
$ docker service rm logging_logstash
$ docker config rm logging_logstash.conf
$ docker stack deploy logging -c compose-logging.yml
```

Docker configs are immutable objects inside a Docker Swarm cluster. This is why we had to recreate the Logstash service.

3. Now that we have our new logging stack, let us rerun our benchmark:

```
$ jmeter -n -t benchmark.jmx
```

Now that we have extracted the response times from our Ruby application, we can plot these data points in a Kibana visualization. The following is a screenshot of Kibana showing the average response time per second of the benchmark we ran earlier:

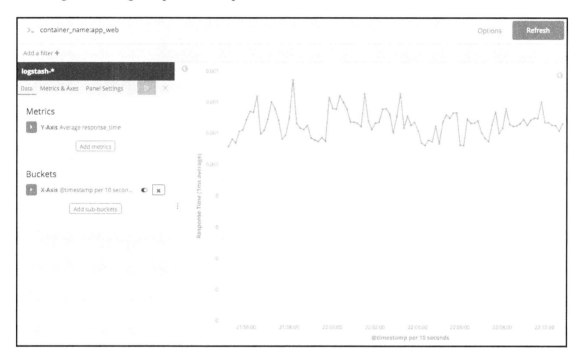

Another result we can explore is how the CPU usage of our application responded to our benchmark. We can make the following Prometheus query in our Grafana dashboard:

```
rate(
 container_cpu_user_seconds_total{
 container_label_com_docker_swarm_service_name="app_web"
 }
[1m])
+ rate(
 container_cpu_system_seconds_total{
 container_label_com_docker_swarm_service_name="app_web"
 }
[1m])
```

As we can see in the following graph, the CPU increased the moment our application started receiving requests:

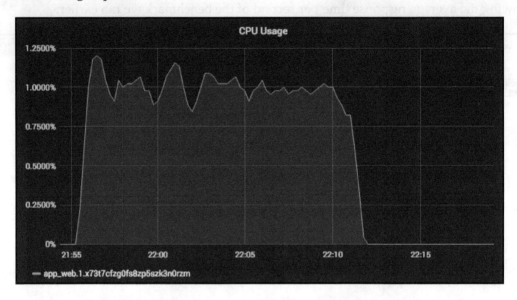

We can explore other system measurements of our Docker Swarm cluster to see how it is affected by the load of HTTP requests that it gets. The important point is that we use this data and correlate it to see how our web application behaves.

Tuning the benchmark

At this point, we already have a basic workflow of creating a test plan in Apache JMeter and analyzing the preliminary results. From here, there are several parameters we can adjust to achieve our benchmark objectives. In this section, we will iterate on our test plan to identify the limits of our Docker application.

Increasing concurrency

The first parameter that we may want to tune is increase **Loop Count** of our test plan. Driving our test plan to generate more requests will allow us to see the effects of the load we induced on our application. This increases the precision of our benchmark experiments, because outlier events such as a slow network connection or hardware failure (unless we are testing that specifically!) affect our tests.

After having enough data points for our benchmarks, we may realize that the load being generated is not enough against our Docker application. For example, the current throughput we received from our first analysis may not simulate the behavior of real users. Let's say that we want to have 2,000 requests per second. To increase the rate at which JMeter generates the requests, we can increase the **Number of Threads** in the thread group that we created earlier. This increases the number of concurrent requests that JMeter is creating at a time. If we want to simulate a gradual increase in the number of users, we can adjust the **Ramp-up Period** to be longer.

 For workloads where we want to simulate a sudden increase of users, we can stick with a **Ramp-up Period** of 0 to start all of the threads right away. In cases where we want to tune other behaviors, such as a constant load and then a sudden spike, we can use the **Stepping Thread Group** plugin.

We may also want to limit it to precisely just five requests per second. Here, we can use `Timer` elements to control how our threads generate the request. To start limiting throughput, we can use the **Constant Throughput Timer**. This will make JMeter automatically slow down threads when it detects that the throughput it is receiving from our web application is increasing too much.

Some of the benchmark techniques here are difficult to apply with the built-in Apache JMeter components. There are a variety of plugins that make it simpler to generate the load to drive our application. The Apache JMeter list of popularly used community plugins is at `http://jmeter-plugins.org`.

Running distributed tests

After tuning the concurrency parameters for a while, we will come to realize that our result does not change. We may set JMeter to generate 10,000 requests at a time, but that will most likely crash our JMeter session! In this case, we are already reaching the performance limits of our workstation when running the benchmarks. From this point onward, we can start using a pool of servers that run JMeter to create distributed tests. Distributed tests are useful because we can grab several servers from the cloud with higher performance to simulate spikes. It is also useful for creating load coming from several sources. This distributed setup is useful for simulating high-latency scenarios, where our users are accessing our Docker application from halfway across the world.

Go through the following steps to deploy Apache JMeter on several Docker hosts to perform a distributed benchmark:

1. First, create the following `Dockerfile` to create a Docker image called `hubuser/jmeter`:

```
FROM openjdk:11-jre-stretch

RUN curl -s
https://www.apache.org/dist/jmeter/binaries/apache-jmeter-5.1.tgz\
| tar xz

ADD benchmark.jmx /jmeter/benchmark.jmx

WORKDIR /jmeter
RUN /apache-jmeter-5.1/bin/create-rmi-keystore.sh -dname\
'CN=jmeter'

EXPOSE 1099
EXPOSE 1100

ENTRYPOINT ["/apache-jmeter-5.1/bin/jmeter"]

CMD ["-j", "/dev/stdout", "-s", \
     "-Dserver_port=1099", "-Jserver_rmi_localport=1100"]
```

2. Next, build the Docker image and publish it to Docker Hub, using the following code:

```
dockerhost$ docker build -t hubuser/jmeter .
dockerhost$ docker push hubuser/jmeter
```

3. Now that our Docker image is published, let's now create a JMeter service with two replicas in a compose file called `compose-jmeter.yml`, using the following code:

```
---
version: '3.7'

services:
  jmeter:
    image: hubuser/jmeter

    deploy:
      replicas: 2
      endpoint_mode: dnsrr
```

```
networks:
  default:
    driver: overlay
    attachable: true
```

Note that we also set `endpoint_mode: dnsrr` in our service, as we don't need a virtual IP address for our JMeter service. We will connect to each replica one by one from our JMeter client session later.

4. Now that the definition of our service is ready, let's deploy it to our Docker Swarm cluster using the following code:

```
dockerhost$ docker stack deploy benchmark -c compose-benchmark.yml
```

5. Once the JMeter service is running, let's determine the IP addresses of each replica by making the following DNS query against its Docker overlay network `benchmark_default`:

```
dockerhost$ docker run --network=benchmark_default --rm alpine
nslookup jmeter
...
Name:      jmeter
Address 1: 10.0.4.3
benchmark_jmeter.2.11ybjbcroa3sn20yfn2i2klzc.benchmark_default
Address 2: 10.0.4.2
benchmark_jmeter.1.vpth5fzhz5dsg2w1ic0bbpf84.benchmark_default
```

In our preceding query, the IP addresses of the replicas are `10.0.4.2` and `10.0.4.3`.

6. To run our JMeter benchmark remotely through these running JMeter servers, let's invoke JMeter with the `-R` option indicating the IP addresses of each service, using the following code:

```
dockerhost$ docker run --network=benchmark_default  --entrypoint
/bin/sh -it aespinosa/jmeter
# /apache-jmeter-5.1/bin/jmeter -n -t benchmark.jmx -R
10.0.4.3,10.0.4.2
...
Configuring remote engine: 10.0.4.3
Configuring remote engine: 10.0.4.2
Starting remote engines
Starting the test @ Sat Mar 09 15:11:01 UTC 2019 (1552144261705)
...
summary =  20000 in 00:00:26 =  766.9/s Avg:     1 Min:     0 Max:
```

```
20041 Err: 10000 (50.00%)
Tidying up remote @ Sat Mar 09 15:11:31 UTC 2019 (1552144291696)
... end of run
...
```

In our original benchmark with 10,000 tests, a distributed test ran the same 10,000 on each replica, making a total of `20000` requests for our application. We can also see this by counting the number of lines in the resulting data that was generated, as shown in the following code:

```
# wc -l result.jtl
20001 result.jtl
```

 More information on distributed and remote testing can be found at `http://jmeter.apache.org/usermanual/remote-test.html`.

Other benchmarking tools

There are a few other benchmarking tools specifically for benchmarking web-based applications. The following is a short list of such tools, along with their links:

- **Apache Bench**: `http://httpd.apache.org/docs/2.4/en/programs/ab.html`
- **HP Lab's httperf**: `https://github.com/httperf/httperf`
- **Siege**: `https://www.joedog.org/siege-home`

Summary

In this chapter, we created benchmarks for gauging the performance of our Docker application. By using Apache JMeter and the monitoring system we set up in `Chapter 3`, *Monitoring Docker*, we analyzed how our application behaved under various conditions. We now have an idea about the limitations of our application and will use this to further optimize it or to scale it out.

In the next chapter, we will talk about load balancers for scaling out our application to increase its capacity.

7
Load Balancing

No matter how we tune our Docker applications, we will reach our application's performance limits. Using the benchmarking techniques we discussed in the previous chapter, we should be able to identify the capacity of our application. In the near future, our Docker application's users will exceed this limit. We cannot turn these users away just because our Docker application cannot handle their requests anymore. We need to scale out our application so that it can serve our growing number of users.

In this chapter, we will talk about how to scale out our Docker applications to increase our capacity. We will use load balancers, which are a key component in the architecture of various web scale applications. Load balancers distribute our application's users to multiple Docker applications deployed in our farm of Docker hosts. The following steps covered in this chapter will help us to accomplish this:

- Preparing application backends
- Balancing load with NGINX
- Scaling out with Docker
- Deploying with zero downtime

Preparing application backends

To create a load balanced application, we must first prepare the application where it is served by several replicas in our Docker Swarm service. In the following steps, we will deploy an application that is scaled in our Docker Swarm cluster:

1. First, we will provision additional nodes in our Docker Swarm cluster. This is to make sure we have enough capacity in our cluster to scale out our application later. In the following output, we can see that we have four nodes available:

```
dockerhost$ docker node ls
ID            HOSTNAME      STATUS AVAILA...  MANAGER...  ENGINE VERSION
9tcxzq45 * dockerhost Ready   Active     Leader      18.09.3
thxcn7ev      node-51fg   Ready   Active                 18.09.0
71yr93qf      node-ftc0   Ready   Active                 18.09.0
oydrnufp      node-hqvv   Ready   Active                 18.09.0
```

2. Next, we will prepare a simple Node.js application in a file called `app.js`. The following app logs additional information related on how our application is load balanced across multiple replicas:

```
var http = require('http');

var server = http.createServer(function (request, response) {
    response.writeHead(200, {"Content-Type": "text/plain"});
    var version = "1.0.0";
    var log = {};
    log.header = 'mywebapp';
    log.name = process.env.HOSTNAME;
    log.version = version;
    console.log(JSON.stringify(log));
    response.end(version + " Hello World  "+ process.env.HOSTNAME);
});
server.listen(8000);
```

3. To deploy the preceding application code, we will package it in a Docker image called `hubuser/app:1.0.0` with the following `Dockerfile`:

```
FROM node:11-stretch

COPY app.js /app/app.js
EXPOSE 8000
CMD ["node", "/app/app.js"]
```

4. Make sure that our Docker image is built and available at Docker Hub. This way, we can easily deploy it. Run this with the following command:

```
dockerhost$ docker build -t hubuser/app:1.0.0 .
dockerhost$ docker push hubuser/app:1.0.0
```

5. Next, let's create the definition of our application service in a compose file called `compose-lb.yml`:

```
---
version: '3.7'

services:
  app_green:
    image: hubuser/app:1.0.0
    deploy:
      replicas: 2
      endpoint_mode: dnsrr

networks:
  default:
    aliases:
      - application
```

Note that we set our application to run at two replicas. We also made an additional alias for our service called `application`. Finally, we set the use of DNS round-robin as the endpoint mode as we will load balance it with NGINX later.

6. Finally, let's deploy our service:

```
dockerhost$ docker stack deploy balancing -c compose-lb.yml
```

Our application is now ready to serve traffic. In the next section, we will configure NGINX to load balance traffic to these replicas.

Balancing load with NGINX

Now that we have a pool of Docker applications to forward traffic to, we can prepare our load balancer. In this section, we will briefly cover NGINX, a popular web server that has high concurrency and performance. It is commonly used as a reverse proxy to forward requests to more dynamic web applications, such as the Node.js one we wrote earlier. By configuring NGINX to have multiple reverse proxy destinations, such as our pool of Docker applications, it will balance the load of requests coming to it across the pool.

The following steps will deploy NGINX to our Docker Swarm cluster for load balancing:

1. First, let's prepare an NGINX configuration file called `nginx.conf`:

```
events { }

http {
   resolver 127.0.0.11 valid=5s ipv6=off;

   server {
     listen 80;
     location / {
       set $backend application;
       proxy_pass http://$backend:8000;
     }
   }
}
```

Note that we used NGINX's DNS service discovery to send traffic to our application via its network alias `application`.

2. Next, let's update our `compose-lb.yml` compose file to include our NGINX service. This will be the ingress point to our application:

```
---
version: '3.7'

services:
  nginx: # Add this new nginx service
    image: nginx:stable
    ports:
      - '80:80'
    configs:
      - source: nginx.conf
        target: /etc/nginx/nginx.conf
  app_green:
    image: hubuser/app:1.0.0
    deploy:
      replicas: 2
      endpoint_mode: dnsrr

configs: # Include this config
  nginx.conf:
  file: ./nginx.conf
```

3. Finally, let's deploy our NGINX service by updating our stack deployment:

```
dockerhost$ docker stack deploy balancing -c compose-lb.yml
```

Our web application is now accessible via http://dockerhost (or any port 80 of each Docker Swarm node). Each request will then be routed to one of the hubuser/webapp:1.0.0 replicas deployed to our Docker Swarm cluster.

To confirm our deployment, we can look at our Kibana visualization to show the distribution of traffic across our three hosts. To show the distribution of traffic, we must first generate a load for our application. We can use our JMeter testing infrastructure described in Chapter 6, *Benchmarking*, to achieve this. For quick testing, we can also generate a load using a long-running command similar to the following:

```
$ while true; do curl http://dockerhost && sleep 0.1; done
1.0.0 Hello World   56547aceb063
1.0.0 Hello World   af272c6968f0
1.0.0 Hello World   56547aceb063
1.0.0 Hello World   af272c6968f0
1.0.0 Hello World   56547aceb063
1.0.0 Hello World   af272c6968f0
```

Recall that, in the application we prepared earlier, we printed out $HOSTNAME as a part of the HTTP response. In the preceding case, the responses show the Docker container's hostname. Note that Docker containers get the short hash of their container IDs as their hostname by default. As we can note from the initial output of our test workload, we are getting responses from three containers.

We can visualize the response better in a Kibana visualization if we set up our logging infrastructure as we did in Chapter 3, *Monitoring Docker*.

In the following screenshot, we can count the number of responses per minute according to the Docker host that the log entry came from:

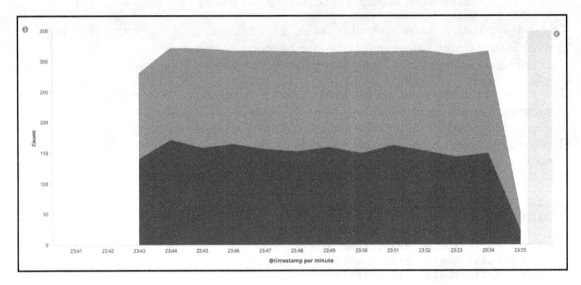

We can note in the preceding graph that our workload gets distributed evenly by NGINX to our application's two replicas.

Scaling out our Docker applications

Now, suppose that the workload in the previous section starts to overload each of our three Docker hosts. Without a load balancer such as our preceding NGINX setup, our application's performance will start to degrade. This may mean a lower quality of service to our application's users or being paged in the middle of the night to perform heroic systems operations. However, with a load balancer managing the connections to our applications, it is very simple to add more capacity to scale out the performance of our application.

As our application is already designed to be load balanced, our scale-out process is very simple. The only thing we need to do is update the number of replicas of our application in the `compose-lb.yml` file:

```
---
version: '3.7'

services:
  nginx:
    image: nginx:stable
```

```
    ports:
      - '80:80'
    configs:
      - source: nginx.conf
        target: /etc/nginx/nginx.conf
  app_green:
    image: hubuser/app:1.0.0
    deploy:
      replicas: 4 # Update this replica number
      endpoint_mode: dnsrr
    networks:
      default:
        aliases:
          - application

# configs: ...
```

After that, we then update our deployment:

```
dockerhost$ docker stack deploy balancing -c compose-lb.yml
```

Now that we are done scaling out our Docker application, let's look back at our Kibana visualization to observe the effect. The following screenshot shows the distribution of traffic across the five Docker hosts we currently have:

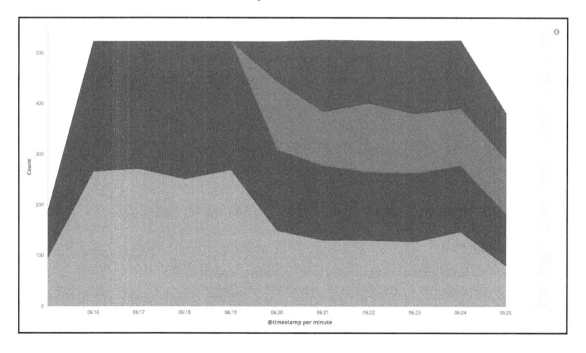

We can note in the preceding screenshot that, after we reloaded NGINX, it started to distribute the load across our new Docker containers. Before this, each Docker container received only half of the traffic from NGINX. Now, each Docker application in the pool only receives a quarter of the traffic.

Deploying with zero downtime

Another advantage of having our Docker application load balanced is that we can use the same load-balancing techniques to update our application. Normally, operations engineers have to schedule downtime or a maintenance window in order to update an application deployed in production. However, as our application's traffic goes to a load balancer before it reaches our application, we can use this intermediate step to our advantage. In this section, we will employ a technique called blue-green deployments to update our running application with zero downtime.

Our current pool of `hubuser/app:1.0.0` Docker containers is called our green Docker host pool because it actively receives requests from our NGINX load balancer. We will update the application being served by our NGINX load balancer to a pool of `hubuser/app:2.0.0` Docker containers. The following are the steps to perform the update:

1. First, let's update our application by changing the `version` string in our `app.js` file, as follows:

```
var http = require('http');

var server = http.createServer(function (request, response) {
  response.writeHead(200, {"Content-Type": "text/plain"});
  var version = "2.0.0";
// ...
});

server.listen(8000);
```

2. After updating the content, we will prepare a new version of our Docker image called `hubuser/app:2.0.0` and publish it to Docker Hub via the following command:

```
dockerhost$ docker build -t hubuser/app:2.0.0 .
dockerhost$ docker push hubuser/app:2.0.0
```

3. Optionally, we can add more Docker Swarm worker nodes, if we think more capacity is needed to run more containers.

4. Next, let's update our compose file to deploy the new version of our service. We will name this service `app_blue` and deploy it alongside our original service:

```
---
version: '3.7'

services:
  nginx:
    image: nginx:stable
    ports:
      - '80:80'
    configs:
      - source: nginx.conf
        target: /etc/nginx/nginx.conf
  app_green:
    image: hubuser/app:1.0.0
    deploy:
      replicas: 4
      endpoint_mode: dnsrr
    networks:
      default:
        aliases:
          - application
  app_blue: # Add this new applicaiton
    image: hubuser/app:2.0.0
    deploy:
      replicas: 2
      endpoint_mode: dnsrr

configs:
  nginx.conf:
    file: ./nginx.conf
```

5. Next, we deploy and update to our stack:

```
dockerhost$ docker stack deploy balancing -c compose-lb.yml
```

Our blue application replicas are now running. It is called blue because, although it is now live and running, it has yet to receive user traffic. At this point, we can do whatever is needed, such as perform preflight checks and tests before siphon our users to the new version of our application.

6. After we are confident that our blue application service is fully functional and working, it is time to send traffic to it. To accomplish this, we will add the network alias, `application`, to the new version of our service by updating `compose-lb.yml` again:

```
---
version: '3.7'

services:
# nginx: ...
# app_green: ...
  app_blue:
    # ...
    networks:
      default:
        aliases:
          - application

# configs: ...
```

7. To complete the update, let's deploy our stack again:

dockerhost$ docker stack deploy balancing -c compose-lb.yml

At this point, NGINX sends traffic to both the old version (`hubuser/app:1.0.0`) and the new version (`hubuser/app:2.0.0`) of our Docker application. With this, we can completely verify that our new application is indeed working as expected because it now serves live traffic from our application's users. In the cases when it does not work properly, we can safely roll back by removing the network alias in our blue application service and update our deployment.

8. However, suppose we are already satisfied with our new application. We can then safely remove the old Docker application from our load balancer's configuration. To do this, let's scale our application to zero replicas:

```
---
version: '3.7'

services:
  nginx:
    image: nginx:stable
    ports:
      - '80:80'
    configs:
      - source: nginx.conf
        target: /etc/nginx/nginx.conf
```

```
  app_green:
    image: hubuser/app:1.0.0
    deploy:
      replicas: 4
      endpoint_mode: dnsrr
    networks:
      default:
        aliases:
          - application
  app_blue:
    image: hubuser/app:2.0.0
    deploy:
      replicas: 2
      endpoint_mode: dnsrr
    networks: # Add this new network alias
      default:
        aliases:
          - application

configs:
  nginx.conf:
    file: ./nginx.conf
```

9. And finally, let's deploy our stack one last time:

```
dockerhost$ docker stack deploy balancing -c compose-lb.yml
```

Congratulations! We finished the blue-green deployment of our new application and we did it with zero downtime! At this point, our blue application service serves all of the production traffic of our application.

The whole blue-green deployment process we undertook earlier can be summarized in the following Kibana visualization:

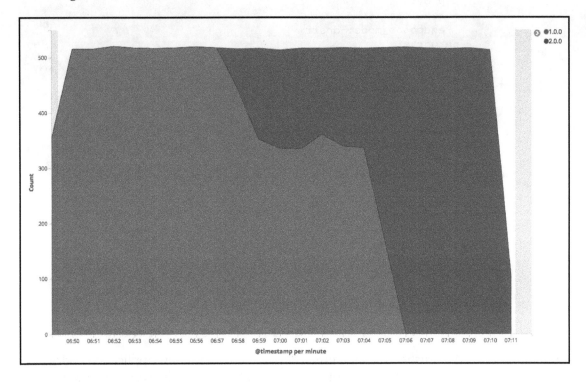

Note that, in the preceding graph, our application still serves traffic even though we updated our application. Note also that, before this, all of the traffic was distributed to our four **1.0.0** applications. After activating the blue Docker host pool, a third of the traffic started going to Version **2.0.0** of our application. In the end, we deactivated all of the endpoints in our old green application service, and all of the application's traffic is now served by Version **2.0.0** of our application.

More information about blue-green deployments and other types of zero-downtime release techniques can be found in a book called *Continuous Delivery* by Jez Humble and Dave Farley. The book's website can be found at http://continuousdelivery.com.

Other load balancers

There are other tools that can be used to load balance applications. Some are similar to NGINX, where configuration is defined through external configuration files. Then, we can send a signal to the running process to reload the updated configuration. Some have their pool configurations stored in an outside store, such as Redis, etcd, and even regular databases, so that the list is dynamically loaded by the load balancer itself. Even NGINX has some of these functionalities in its commercial offering. There are also other open source projects that extend NGINX with third-party modules.

The following is a short list of load balancers that we can deploy as some form of Docker containers in our infrastructure:

- HAProxy (`http://www.haproxy.org`)
- Apache HTTP Server (`http://httpd.apache.org`)
- Traefik (`https://traefik.io/`)

There are also hardware-based load balancers that we can procure ourselves and configure via their own proprietary formats or APIs. If we use cloud providers, some of their own load balancer offerings would have their own cloud APIs that we can use as well.

Summary

In this chapter, we learned about the benefits of using load balancers and how to use them. We deployed and configured NGINX as a load balancer in a Docker container so that we could scale out our Docker application. We also used the load balancer to perform zero-downtime releases to update our application to a new version.

In the next chapter, we will continue to improve our Docker optimization skills by debugging inside the Docker containers we deploy.

8
Troubleshooting Containers

Sometimes, setting up instrumentation such as the monitoring and logging system (like we did in `Chapter 3`, *Monitoring Docker*) might not be enough. Ideally, we should create a way to troubleshoot our Docker deployments in a scalable fashion. However, sometimes, we have no choice but to log in to the Docker host and look at the Docker containers themselves. It is important to know how to interact with our Docker hosts in order to figure out what is going on with our systems. These low-level debugging activities will also help to improve our monitoring and logging system for our Docker infrastructure.

In this chapter, we will cover the following topics:

- Inspecting containers with the `docker exec` command
- Debugging from outside Docker
- Other container debugging tools

Inspecting containers with the docker exec command

When troubleshooting servers, the traditional way to debug is to log in and poke around the machine. With Docker, this typical workflow is split into two steps: the first is logging in to the Docker host using standard remote access tools such as SSH, and the second is entering the desired running container's process namespace with the `docker exec` command. This is useful as a last resort to debug what is happening inside our application.

For most of this chapter, we will troubleshoot and debug a Docker container running HAProxy. The following steps will prepare the sample container service:

1. First, we will create the configuration for HAProxy named `haproxy.cfg` with the following content:

```
defaults
  mode http
  timeout connect 5000ms
  timeout client 50000ms
  timeout server 50000ms

frontend stats
  bind 127.0.0.1:80
  stats enable

listen http-in
  bind *:80
  server server1 www.debian.org:80
```

2. Next, we will prepare a Compose file, `compose.yml`, describing how to run the HAProxy service:

```
---
version: '3.7'

services:
  haproxy:
    image: haproxy:1.9
    ports:
      - '80:80'
    configs:
      - source: haproxy.cfg
        target: /usr/local/etc/haproxy/haproxy.cfg

configs:
  haproxy.cfg:
    file: ./haproxy.cfg
```

3. Finally, let's run HAProxy by deploying our Docker Compose file:

```
dockerhost$ docker stack deploy haproxy -c compose.yml
```

We can now begin to inspect our container and debug it, which is a good way to confirm that the HAProxy container is listening to port 80. The ss program dumps a summary of sockets statistics available in most Linux distributions, such as our CentOS Docker host. However, since most Docker images are packaged to be as small as possible, debugging programs such as ss may not be available. In the following example, entering our running haproxy container using docker exec tells us that this program is indeed unavailable:

```
dockerhost$ service=$(docker service ps haproxy_haproxy -q)
dockerhost$ docker exec haproxy_haproxy.1.$service ss -l
OCI runtime exec failed: exec failed: container_linux.go:344: starting
container process caused "exec: \"/bin/ss\": stat /bin/ss: no such file or
directory": unknown
```

We can provide a quick workaround by installing it inside our container, similar to what we do in a normal operating system environment. While we are still inside the container, we will type the following command to install ss:

```
dockerhost$ service=$(docker service ps haproxy_haproxy -q)
dockerhost$ docker exec -it haproxy_haproxy.1.$service /bin/bash
# haproxy uses Debian as the base image so we have to use apt for
# installing packages.
root@b397ffb9df13:/# apt-get update
root@b397ffb9df13:/# apt-get install -y iproute2
```

When using the docker ps <service-name> -q command, we can add the --filter desired-state=running flag if the service restarted a few times prior.

We can now run the ss program and confirm that the haproxy service is listening to port 80:

```
root@b397ffb9df13:/# # ss -l -A tcp
State       Recv-Q   Send-Q   Local Address:Port        Peer Address:Port
LISTEN      0        128               *:80                    *:*
LISTEN      0        128      127.0.0.1:80                     *:*
LISTEN      0        128      127.0.0.11:41372                 *:*
```

This approach of ad hoc container debugging is not recommended! Logging in to Docker hosts manually may introduce unintended changes to our infrastructure that we didn't expect. This will make debugging even harder in the future.

The following are some limitations of this last-resort approach:

- When we stop and recreate the container, the netstat package we installed will not be available anymore. This is because the original HAProxy Docker image doesn't contain it in the first place. Installing ad hoc packages to run containers undermines the main feature of Docker, which is to enable an immutable infrastructure.

- In case we want to package all of the debugging tools inside our Docker image, its size will increase correspondingly. This means that our deployments will get larger and become slower. Remember that, in Chapter 4, *Optimizing Docker Images*, we optimized to reduce our container's size.

- In the case of minimal containers with just the required binaries, we are now mostly blind. The bash shell is not even available! There is no way to enter our container; take a look at the following command:

```
dockerhost$ docker exec -it minimal_image /bin/bash
OCI runtime exec failed: exec failed: container_linux.go:344:
starting container process caused "exec: \"/bin/bash\": stat
/bin/bash: no such file or directory": unknown
```

In short, docker exec is a powerful tool that gets inside our containers and debugs by running various commands. Coupled with the -it flags, we can get an interactive shell to perform deeper debugging. This approach has limitations because it assumes that all of the tools available inside our Docker container are ready to use.

 More information about the docker exec command can be found in the official documentation at https://docs.docker.com/engine/reference/commandline/exec/.

After debugging our application with the docker exec command, we should use these lessons to improve the monitoring and logging system we built in Chapter 3, *Monitoring Docker*.

The next section deals with how to get around this limitation by having tools from outside Docker for inspecting the state of our running container. We will provide a brief overview of how to use some of these tools.

Debugging from outside Docker

Even though Docker isolates the network, memory, CPU, and storage resources inside containers, each individual container will still have to go to the Docker host's operating system to perform the actual command. We can take advantage of this trickling down of calls to the host operating system to intercept and debug our Docker containers from the outside. In this section, we will cover some selected tools and how to use them to interact with our Docker containers. We can perform the interaction from the Docker host itself or from inside a sibling container with elevated privileges to see some components of the Docker host.

Tracing system calls

A system call tracer is one of the essential tools for server operations. It is a utility that intercepts and traces calls made by the application to the operating system. Each operating system has its own variation. Even if we run various applications and processes inside our Docker containers, it will eventually enter our Docker host's Linux operating system as a series of system calls.

On Linux systems, the `strace` program is used to trace these system calls. This interception and logging functionality of `strace` can be used to inspect our Docker containers from the outside. The list of system calls made throughout our container's lifetime can give a profile-level view of how it behaves.

To get started using `strace`, simply type the following command to install it inside our CentOS Docker host:

```
dockerhost$ yum install -y
```

With the `--pid=host` option added to the `docker run` command, we can set a container's PID namespace to be of the Docker host's. This way, we'll be able to install and use `strace` inside a Docker container to inspect all of the processes in the Docker host itself. We can also install `strace` from a different Linux distribution, such as Ubuntu, if we use the corresponding base image for our container.

More information describing this option is at `http://docs.docker.com/engine/reference/run/#pid-settings---pid`.

Now that we have `strace` installed in our Docker host, we can use it to inspect the system calls inside the HAProxy container we created in the previous section. Type the following commands to begin tracing the system calls from the HAProxy container:

```
dockerhost$ service=$(docker service ps haproxy_haproxy -q)
dockerhost$ container=haproxy_haproxy.1.$service
dockerhost$ pid=$(docker inspect -f '{{.State.Pid}}' $container)
dockerhost$ strace -p $(pgrep -P $pid)
clock_gettime(CLOCK_THREAD_CPUTIME_ID, {0, 251877895}) = 0
clock_gettime(CLOCK_THREAD_CPUTIME_ID, {0, 251931556}) = 0
epoll_wait(4, [], 200, 1000)           = 0
clock_gettime(CLOCK_THREAD_CPUTIME_ID, {0, 252169242}) = 0
clock_gettime(CLOCK_THREAD_CPUTIME_ID, {0, 252263388}) = 0
epoll_wait(4, [], 200, 1000)           = 0
clock_gettime(CLOCK_THREAD_CPUTIME_ID, {0, 252505040}) = 0
clock_gettime(CLOCK_THREAD_CPUTIME_ID, {0, 252600407}) = 0
epoll_wait(4, [], 200, 1000)
...
```

As you can see, our HAProxy container makes `epoll_wait()` calls to wait for incoming network connections. Now, in a separate Terminal, type the following command to make an HTTP request to our running container:

```
$ curl http://dockerhost
```

Now, let's go back to our running `strace` program earlier. We can see the following lines printed out:

```
...
epoll_wait(5, [{EPOLLIN, {u32=7, u64=7}}], 200, 1000) = 1
clock_gettime(CLOCK_THREAD_CPUTIME_ID, {0, 262270237}) = 0
accept4(7, {sa_family=AF_INET, sin_port=htons(63212),
sin_addr=inet_addr("10.255.0.2")}, [16], SOCK_NONBLOCK) = 10
setsockopt(10, SOL_TCP, TCP_NODELAY, [1], 4) = 0
accept4(7, 0x7fff262ba090, 0x7fff262ba084, SOCK_NONBLOCK) = -1 EAGAIN
(Resource temporarily unavailable)
recvfrom(10, "GET / HTTP/1.1\r\nUser-Agent: curl"..., 15360, 0, NULL, NULL)
= 75
socket(AF_INET, SOCK_STREAM, IPPROTO_TCP) = 11
fcntl(11, F_SETFL, O_RDONLY|O_NONBLOCK) = 0
setsockopt(11, SOL_TCP, TCP_NODELAY, [1], 4) = 0
connect(11, {sa_family=AF_INET, sin_port=htons(80),
sin_addr=inet_addr("149.20.4.15")}, 16) = -1 EINPROGRESS (Operation now in
progress)
sendto(11, "GET / HTTP/1.1\r\nUser-Agent: curl"..., 75,
MSG_DONTWAIT|MSG_NOSIGNAL, NULL, 0) = -1 EAGAIN (Resource temporarily
unavailable)
```

```
epoll_ctl(5, EPOLL_CTL_ADD, 11, {EPOLLOUT, {u32=11, u64=11}}) = 0
...
```

We can see here that HAProxy made standard BSD-style socket system calls, such as `accept4()`, `socket()`, and `close()`, to accept, process, and terminate network connections from our HTTP client. Finally, it goes back to `epoll_wait()` again to wait for the next connections. Also, take note that `epoll_wait()` calls are spread throughout the trace even while HAProxy processes a connection. This shows how HAProxy can handle concurrent connections.

Tracing system calls is a very useful technique to debug live production systems. People in operations sometimes get paged and don't have access to the source code right away. Alternatively, there are instances where we are only given compiled binaries (or plain Docker images) running in production where there is no source code (nor `Dockerfile`). The only clue we can get from a running application is to trap the system calls it makes to the Linux kernel.

> The `strace` web page can be found at `https://strace.io/`. More information can be accessed through its `man` page, as well, by typing the following command:
>
> **dockerhost$ man 1 strace**
>
> For a more comprehensive list of system calls in Linux systems, refer to `http://man7.org/linux/man-pages/man2/syscalls.2.html`. This will be useful in understanding the various outputs given by `strace`.

Analyzing network packets

Most Docker containers that we deploy revolve around providing some form of network service. In the example of HAProxy in this chapter, our container basically serves HTTP network traffic. No matter what kind of container we have running, the network packets will eventually have to get out of the Docker host for it to complete a request that we send it. By dumping and analyzing the content of these packets, we can gain some insight into the nature of our Docker container. In this section, we will use a packet analyzer called `tcpdump` to view the traffic of network packets being received and sent by our Docker containers.

To begin using `tcpdump`, we can issue the following command in our CentOS Docker host to install it:

```
dockerhost$ yum install -y tcpdump
```

We can also expose the Docker host's network interfaces to a container. With this approach, we can install `tcpdump` in a container and not pollute our main Docker host with ad hoc debugging packages. This can be done by specifying the `--net=host` flag on the `docker run` command. With this, we can access the `docker0` interface from inside our Docker container with `tcpdump`.

The example of using `tcpdump` will be very specific to the Vagrant VMware Fusion provider for VMware Fusion 7.0. Assuming we have a Docker CentOS host as a Vagrant VMware Fusion box, run the following command to suspend and unsuspend our Docker host's virtual machine:

```
$ vagrant suspend
$ vagrant up
$ vagrant ssh
dockerhost$
```

Now that we are back inside our Docker host, run the following command and note that we cannot resolve `www.google.com` anymore inside our interactive `debian:jessie` container, as follows:

```
dockerhost$ docker run -it debian:jessie /bin/bash
root@fce09c8c0e16:/# ping www.google.com
ping: unknown host
```

Now, let's run `tcpdump` in a separate Terminal. While running the preceding `ping` command, we will notice the following output from our `tcpdump` Terminal:

```
dockerhost$ tcpdump -i docker0
tcpdump: verbose output suppressed, use -v or -vv for full protocol decode
listening on docker0, link-type EN10MB (Ethernet), capture size 262144
bytes
22:03:34.512942 ARP, Request who-has 172.17.42.1 tell 172.17.0.7, length 28
22:03:35.512931 ARP, Request who-has 172.17.42.1 tell 172.17.0.7, length 28
22:03:38.520681 ARP, Request who-has 172.17.42.1 tell 172.17.0.7, length 28
22:03:39.520099 ARP, Request who-has 172.17.42.1 tell 172.17.0.7, length 28
22:03:40.520927 ARP, Request who-has 172.17.42.1 tell 172.17.0.7, length 28
22:03:43.527069 ARP, Request who-has 172.17.42.1 tell 172.17.0.7, length 28
```

As we can see, the interactive `/bin/bash` container is looking for `172.17.42.1`, which is normally the IP address attached to the Docker Engine network device, `docker0`. With this figured out, take a look at `docker0` by typing the following command:

```
dockerhost$ ip addr show dev docker0
3: docker0: <BROADCAST,MULTICAST,UP,LOWER_UP> mtu 1500 qdisc noqueue state
UP group default
    link/ether 02:42:46:66:64:b8 brd ff:ff:ff:ff:ff:ff
    inet6 fe80::42:46ff:fe66:64b8/64 scope link
       valid_lft forever preferred_lft forever
```

Now, we can view the problem. The `docker0` device doesn't have an IPv4 address attached to it. Somehow, VMware unsuspending our Docker host removes the mapped IP address in `docker0`. Fortunately, the solution is to simply restart the Docker Engine, and Docker will reinitialize the `docker0` network interface by itself. Restart Docker Engine by typing the following command in our Docker host:

```
dockerhost$ systemctl restart docker.service
```

Now, when we run the same command as earlier, we will see that the IP address is attached, as follows:

```
dockerhost$ ip addr show dev docker0
3: docker0: <NO-CARRIER,BROADCAST,MULTICAST,UP> mtu 1500 qdisc noque...
    link/ether 02:42:46:66:64:b8 brd ff:ff:ff:ff:ff:ff
    inet 172.17.42.1/16 scope global docker0
       valid_lft forever preferred_lft forever
    inet6 fe80::42:46ff:fe66:64b8/64 scope link
       valid_lft forever preferred_lft forever
```

Let's go back to our initial command showing the problem; we will see that it is now solved, as follows:

```
root@fce09c8c0e16:/# ping www.google.com
PING www.google.com (74.125.21.105): 56 data bytes
64 bytes from 74.125.21.105: icmp_seq=0 ttl=127 time=65.553 ms
64 bytes from 74.125.21.105: icmp_seq=1 ttl=127 time=38.270 ms
...
```

More information about the `tcpdump` packet dumper and analyzer can be found at `http://www.tcpdump.org`. We can also access the documentation from where we installed it by typing the following command:

```
dockerhost$ man 8 tcpdump
```

Observing block devices

Data being accessed from our Docker containers will mostly reside in physical storage devices, such as hard disks or solid state drives. Underneath Docker's copy-on-write filesystems is a physical device that is randomly accessed. These drives are grouped together as block devices. Data here is randomly accessed fixed-size data called blocks.

So, in case our Docker containers have peculiar I/O behavior and performance issues, we can trace and troubleshoot what is happening inside our block devices using a tool called `blktrace`. All events that the kernel generates to interact with the block devices from processes are intercepted by this program. In this section, we will set up our Docker host to observe the block device supporting our containers underneath.

To use `blktrace`, let's prepare our Docker host by installing the `blktrace` program. Type the following command to install it inside our Docker host:

```
dockerhost$ yum install -y blktrace
```

In addition, we need to enable debugging of the filesystem. We can do this by typing the following command in our Docker host:

```
dockerhost$ mount -t debugfs debugfs /sys/kernel/debug
```

After the preparations, we need to figure out how to tell `blktrace` where to listen for I/O events. To trace I/O events for our containers, we need to know where the root of the Docker runtime is. In the default configuration of our Docker host, the runtime points to the `/var/lib/docker` directory. To figure out which partition it belongs to, type the following command:

```
dockerhost$ df -h
Filesystem      Size  Used Avail Use% Mounted on
/dev/sda1        10G  7.2G  2.9G  72% /
devtmpfs        7.3G     0  7.3G   0% /dev
tmpfs           7.3G     0  7.3G   0% /dev/shm
tmpfs           7.3G  8.6M  7.3G   1% /run
tmpfs           7.3G     0  7.3G   0% /sys/fs/cgroup
/dev/sdb        9.8G  159M  9.1G   2% /var/lib/docker/swarm
tmpfs           1.5G     0  1.5G   0% /run/user/0
tmpfs           1.5G     0  1.5G   0% /run/user/1000
```

As described in the preceding output, our Docker host's `/var/lib/docker` directory is under the `/` partition. This is where we will point `blktrace` to listen for events from. Type the following command to start listening for I/O events on this device:

```
dockerhost$ blktrace -d /dev/sda1 -o dump
```

By using the `--privileged` flag in the `docker run` command, we can use `blktrace` within a container. Doing so will allow us to mount the debugged filesystem with the increased privileges.
More information on extended container privileges can be found at `https://docs.docker.com/engine/reference/run/#runtime-privilege-linux-capabilities-and-lxc-configuration`.

To create a simple workload that will generate I/O events in our disk, we will create an empty file from a container until the / partition runs out of free space. Type the following command to generate this workload:

```
dockerhost$ docker run -d --name dump  debian:stretch \
    /bin/dd if=/dev/zero of=/root/dump bs=65000
```

Depending on the free space available in our root partition, this command may finish quickly. Right away, let's get the PID of the container we just ran using the following command:

```
dockerhost$ docker inspect -f '{{.State.Pid}}' dump
11099
```

Now that we know the PID of our Docker container that generated I/O events, we can look this up with the `blktrace` program's complementary tool, `blkparse`. The `blktrace` program only listens for the events in the Linux kernel's block I/O layer and dumps the results on a file. The `blkparse` program is the accompanying tool to view and analyze the events. In the workload we generated earlier, we can look for the I/O events that correspond to our Docker container's PID using the following command:

```
dockerhost$ blkparse -i dump.blktrace.0 | grep " $PID "
...
254,0    0      730    10.6267 11099  Q   R 13667072 + 24 [exe]
254,0    0      732    10.6293 11099  Q   R 5042728 + 16 [exe]
254,0    0      734    10.6299 11099  Q   R 13900768 + 152 [exe]
254,0    0      736    10.6313 11099  Q  RM 4988776 + 8 [exe]
254,0    0     1090    10.671 11099   C   W 11001856 + 1024 [0]
254,0    0     1091    10.6712 11099  C   W 11002880  +  1024  [0]
254,0    0     1092    10.6712 11099  C   W 11003904  +  1024  [0]
254,0    0     1093    10.6712 11099  C   W 11004928  +  1024  [0]
254,0    0     1094    10.6713 11099  C   W 11006976  +  1024  [0]
254,0    0     1095    10.6714 11099  C   W 11005952  +  1024  [0]
254,0    0     1138    10.6930 11099  C   W 11239424  +  1024  [0]
254,0    0     1139    10.6931 11099  C   W 11240448  +  1024  [0]
...
```

In the preceding highlighted output, we can see that the /dev/sda1 block offset the position of 11001856, and there was a writing (W) of 1024 bytes of data that just completed (C). To probe further, we can look at this offset position on the events that it generated. Type the following command to filter out this offset position:

```
dockerhost$ blkparse -i dump.blktrace.0 | grep 11001856
. . .
254,0  0  1066  10.667   8207  Q   W 11001856 + 1024 [kworker/u2:2]
254,0  0  1090  10.671  11099  C   W 11001856 + 1024 [0]
. . .
```

We can see the write (W) being queued (Q) to our device by the kworker process, which means the write was queued by the kernel. After 40 milliseconds, the write request registered was completed for our Docker container process.

The debugging walk-through we just performed is just a small sample of what we can do by tracing block I/O events with blktrace. For example, we can also probe our Docker container's I/O behavior in greater detail and figure out the bottlenecks that are happening to our application. Are there a lot of writes being made? Are the reads so much that they need caching? Having the actual events rather than only the performance metrics provided by the built-in docker stats command is helpful in very deep troubleshooting scenarios.

 More information on the different output values of blkparse and flags to capture I/O events in blktrace, with a copy of its user guide, are located at http://man7.org/linux/man-pages/man8/blktrace.8.html.

Other container debugging tools

Debugging applications inside Docker containers requires a different approach from normal applications in Linux. However, the actual programs being used are the same because all of the calls from inside the container will eventually go to the Docker host's kernel operating system. By knowing how calls go outside of our containers, we can use any other debugging tools we have to troubleshoot.

In addition to standard Linux tools, there are several container-specific utilities that package the preceding standard utilities to be more friendly for container usage. The following are some of these tools:

- Red Hat's `rhel-tools` Docker image is a huge container containing a combination of the tools we discussed earlier. Its documentation page can be found at `https://access.redhat.com/documentation/en-us/red_hat_ enterprise_linux_atomic_host/7/html/managing_containers/running_super_ privileged_containers#using_the_atomic_tools_container_image` shows how to run it with the proper Docker privileges for it to function correctly.
- The CoreOS toolbox program is a small script utility that creates a small Linux container using systemd software's `systemd-nspawn` program. By copying the root filesystem from popular Docker images, we can install any tool we want without polluting the Docker host's filesystem with ad hoc debugging tools. Its use is documented on its web page at `https://coreos.com/os/docs/latest/ install-debugging-tools.html`.

Summary

Remember that logging in to Docker hosts isn't scalable. Adding instrumentation at the application level, in addition to along with the ones given by our operating system, helps with faster and more efficient diagnosing of the problems that we may encounter in the future. Remember, nobody likes waking up at two in the morning to run `tcpdump` to debug a Docker container on fire!

In the next chapter, we will wrap up and look again at what it takes to get our Docker-based workloads to production.

Onto Production 9

Docker came out of dotCloud's PaaS, where it fulfills the needs of IT to develop and deploy web applications in a fast and scalable manner. This is needed to keep up with the ever-accelerating pace of using the web. Keeping everything running in our Docker container in production is no simple feat.

So far, we have learned various details to improve our Docker infrastructure. We learned how to build Docker Swarm clusters automatically. We learned about various systems such as monitoring, logging, and deployment to support our Docker application. We've improved our development and deployment workflow so that our applications are performant and resilient.

In this chapter, we will wrap up what you learned about optimizing Docker and illustrate how it relates to operating our web applications in production. It consists of the following topics:

- Performing web operations
- Supporting our application with Docker
- Deploying applications
- Scaling applications
- Further reading on web operations in general

Performing web operations

Keeping a web application running 24/7 on the internet poses challenges in both software development and systems administration. Docker positions itself as the glue that allows both disciplines to come together by creating Docker images that can be built and deployed in a consistent manner.

However, Docker is not a silver bullet for the web. It is still important to know the fundamental concepts in software development and systems administration as web applications become more complex. The complexity naturally arises because these days, with internet technologies in particular, the multitude of web applications is becoming more ubiquitous in people's lives.

Dealing with the complexity of keeping web applications up and running involves mastering the ins and outs of web operations, and like any road to mastery, Theo Schlossnagle boils it down to four basic pursuits: knowledge, tools, experience, and discipline. *Knowledge* refers to absorbing information about web operations available on the internet and in conferences and technology meetings like a sponge. Understanding them and knowing how to filter out the signal from the noise will aid us in designing our application's architecture when they burn in production. With Docker and Linux containers increasing in popularity, it is important to be aware of the different technologies that support it and dive into its basics. In Chapter 8, *Troubleshooting Containers*, we showed that regular Linux debugging tools are still useful in debugging running Docker containers. By knowing how containers interact with our Docker host's operating system, we were able to debug the problems occurring in Docker.

The second aspect is mastering our tools. This book basically revolved around mastering the use of Docker by looking at how it works and how to optimize its usage. In Chapter 4, *Optimizing Docker Images*, we learned how to optimize Docker images based on how Docker builds the images and runs the container using its copy-on-write filesystem underneath. This was guided by our knowledge of web operations and why optimized Docker images are important both from a scalability and deployability standpoint. Knowing how to use Docker effectively does not happen overnight. Its mastery can only be gained by a continuous practice of using Docker in production. Sure, we might be paged at 2 a.m. for our first Docker deployment in production, but as time goes by, the experience we gain from continuous usage will make Docker an extension of our limbs and senses, as Schlossnagle puts it.

By applying the knowledge and continuously using our tools, we gain experience that we can draw upon in the future. This aids us in making good judgments based on bad decisions that we made in the past. It is the place where we can see the theory of container technology and the practice of running Docker in production collide. Schlossnagle mentioned the challenges of acquiring experience in web operations and how to survive the bad judgments and draw experiences from them. He suggests having limited environments in which a bad decision's impact is minimal. Docker is the best place to draw these types of experiences. Having a standard format of ready-to-deploy Docker images, junior web operations engineers can have their own environments that they can experiment with and in which they can learn from their mistakes. Also, since Docker environments look very similar when they move forward to production, these engineers will already have their experience to draw upon.

The last part in the pursuit of mastering web operations is *discipline*. However, as it is a very young discipline, such processes are not well-defined. Even with Docker, it took a few years for people to realize the best ways to use container technologies. Before this, the convenience of including the whole kitchen sink in Docker images was very common. However, as we can see in Chapter 4, *Optimizing Docker Images*, reducing the footprint of Docker images helps to manage the complexity of the applications that we have to debug. This makes the experience of debugging in Chapter 8, *Troubleshooting Containers*, much simpler because we have fewer components and factors to think about. These disciplines of using Docker do not come overnight just by reading Docker blogs (well, some do). It involves continuous exposure to the knowledge of the Docker community and the practice of using Docker in various settings for production use.

In the remaining sections, we will show how the theory and practice of using Docker's container technology can aid in the operation of our web applications.

Supporting web applications with Docker

The following diagram shows the typical architecture of a web application. We have the load balancer tier that receives traffic from the **Internet** and then the traffic, which is typically composed of user requests, is relayed to a farm of web application servers in a load-balanced fashion.

Depending on the nature of the request, some states will be grabbed by the web application from the persistent storage tier, similar to **Database Servers**:

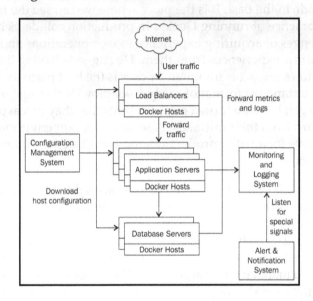

As we can see in the preceding diagram, each tier is run inside a Docker container on top of **Docker Hosts**. With this layout for each component, we can take advantage of Docker's uniform way of deploying load balancers, applications, and databases, as we did in Chapter 2, *Configuring Docker with Chef*, and Chapter 7, *Load Balancing*. However, in addition to the Docker daemons in each Docker host, we need supporting infrastructure to manage and observe the whole stack of our web architecture in a scalable fashion. On the right-hand side, we can see that each of our **Docker Hosts** sends diagnostic information—for example, application and system events such as log messages and metrics—to our centralized logging and monitoring system. We deployed such a system in Chapter 3, *Monitoring Dockers*, where we rolled out Grafana and an ELK stack. In addition, there might be another system that listens for specific signals in the logs and metrics and sends alerts to the engineers responsible for the operation of our Docker-based web application stack. These events can relate to critical events, such as the availability and performance of our application, that we need to take action on to ensure that our application is fulfilling the needs of our business as expected. An internally managed system, such as Nagios, or a third-party one, such as PagerDuty, is used for our Docker deployments to call and wake us up at 2 a.m. for deeper monitoring and troubleshooting sessions as in Chapter 3, *Monitoring Docker*, and Chapter 8, *Troubleshooting Containers*.

The left-hand side of the diagram contains the **Configuration Management System**. This is the place where each of the **Docker Hosts** downloads all of the settings it needs to function properly. In Chapter 2, *Configuring Docker with Chef*, we used a Chef Server to store the configuration of our Docker host. It contained information such as a Docker host's role in our architecture's stack. The Chef Server stores information about which Docker containers to run in each tier and how to run them using the Chef recipes we wrote. Finally, the configuration management system also tells our **Docker Hosts** where the Grafana and Logstash monitoring and logging endpoints are.

All in all, it takes various components to support our web application in production aside from Docker. Docker allows us to set up this infrastructure easily because of the speed and flexibility of deploying containers. Nonetheless, we shouldn't skip doing our homework about having these supporting infrastructures in place. In the next section, we will see the supporting infrastructure of deploying web applications in Docker using the skills you learned in the previous chapters.

Deploying applications

An important component when tuning the performance of Docker containers is the feedback telling us that we were able to improve our web application correctly. The deployment of Graphite and the ELK stack in Chapter 3, *Monitoring Docker*, gave us visibility on the effects of what we changed in our Docker-based web application. As much as it is important to gather feedback, it is more important to gather feedback in a timely manner. Therefore, the deployment of our Docker containers needs to be in a fast and scalable manner. Being able to configure a Docker host automatically, as we did in Chapter 2, *Configuring Docker with Chef*, is an important component for a fast and automated deployment system. The rest of the components are described in the following diagram:

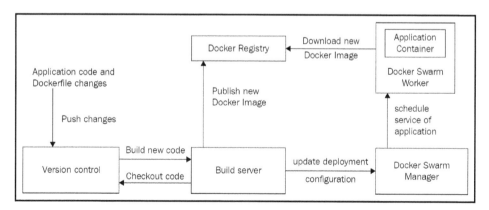

Whenever we submit changes to our application's code or the Dockerfile describing how it is run and built, we need supporting infrastructure to propagate this change all of the way to our Docker hosts. In the preceding diagram, we can see that the changes we submit to our **Version Control** system, such as Git, generate a trigger to build the new version of our code. This is usually done through Git's post-receive hooks in the form of shell scripts. The triggers will be received by a build server, such the Jenkins server that we set up in `Chapter 5`, *Deploying Containers*. The steps to propagate the change will be similar to the blue-green deployment process we made in `Chapter 7`, *Load Balancing*. After receiving the trigger to build the new changes we submitted, Jenkins will take a look at the new version of our code and run `docker build` to create the Docker image. After the build, Jenkins will push the new Docker image to a **Docker Registry**, such as Docker Hub. With new Docker image artifacts available in the **Docker Registry**, our deployment process can now update our service's application definition to use the new versions of our Docker image via a command such as `docker stack deploy`.

In the next section, we will discuss how a similar process is used to scale out our Docker application.

Scaling applications

When we receive alerts from our monitoring system, as in `Chapter 3`, *Monitoring Docker*, that the pool of Docker containers running our web application is not loaded, it is time to scale out. We accomplished this using load balancers in `Chapter 7`, *Load Balancing*. The following diagram shows the high-level architecture of the commands we ran in `Chapter 7`, *Load Balancing*:

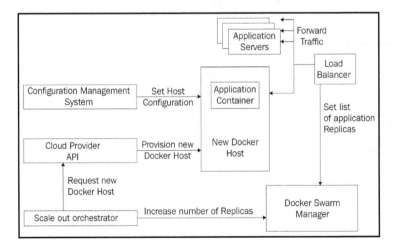

When we decide to scale out and add an additional Docker host, we can automate the process with a **Scale out orchestrator** component. This can be a series of simple shell scripts that we will install inside a build server, such as Jenkins. The orchestrator will basically ask the cloud provider API to create a **New Docker Host**. This request will then provision the Docker host and run the initial bootstrap script to download the configuration from our **Configuration Management System** in Chapter 2, *Configuring Docker with Chef*. This will then increase the number of nodes in our Docker Swarm cluster. After this whole provisioning process is finished, our scale-out orchestrator will then increase the number of replicas of our applications' services. Our NGINX load balancer will start forwarding traffic to these extra replicas.

As we can see from the preceding, learning the way to automate setting up our Docker host in Chapter 2, *Configuring Docker with Chef*, is crucial to realizing the scalable load balancing architecture setup we created in Chapter 7, *Load Balancing*.

Further reading

The supporting architecture to help our web applications to use Docker is nothing but a scratch on the surface. The fundamental concepts in this chapter are described in greater detail in the following books:

- *Web Operations: Keeping the Data On Time*, by J. Allspaw and J. Robbins. 2010 O'Reilly Media
- *Continuous Delivery*, by J. Humble and D. Farley. 2010 Addison-Wesley
- *Jenkins: The Definitive Guide*, by J. F. Smart. 2011 O'Reilly Media
- *The Art of Capacity Planning: Scaling Web Resources*, by J. Allspaw. 2008 O'Reilly Media
- *Pro Git*, by S. Chacon and B. Straub. 2014 Apress

Summary

You learned a lot about how Docker works throughout this book. In addition to the basics of Docker, we looked back at some fundamental concepts of web operations and how they help us to realize the full potential of Docker. You gained knowledge of key Docker and operating systems concepts to get a deeper understanding of what is happening behind the scenes. You now have an idea of how our application goes from our code down to the actual call in the operating system of our Docker host. You learned a lot about the tools to deploy and troubleshoot our Docker containers in production in a scalable and manageable fashion.

However, this should not stop you from continuing to develop and practice using Docker to run web applications in production. We should not be afraid to make mistakes and gain further experience on the best ways to run Docker in production. As the Docker community evolves, so do these practices through the collective experience of the community. So, we should continue and be disciplined about learning the fundamentals we have started to master little by little. Don't hesitate to run Docker in production!

Other Books You May Enjoy

If you enjoyed this book, you may be interested in these other books by Packt:

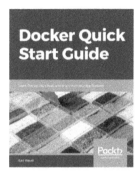

Docker Quick Start Guide
Earl Waud

ISBN: 9781789347326

- Set up your Docker workstation on various platforms
- Utilize a number of Docker commands with parameters
- Create Docker images using Dockerfiles
- Learn how to create and use Docker volumes
- Deploy multi-node Docker swarm infrastructure
- Create and use Docker local and remote networks
- Deploy multi-container applications that are HA and FT
- Use Jenkins to build and deploy Docker images

Docker Cookbook - Second Edition
Ken Cochrane, Jeeva S. Chelladhurai, Neependra K Khare

ISBN: 9781788626866

- Install Docker on various platforms
- Work with Docker images and containers
- Container networking and data sharing
- Docker APIs and language bindings
- Various PaaS solutions for Docker
- Implement container orchestration using Docker Swarm and Kubernetes
- Container security
- Docker on various clouds

Leave a review - let other readers know what you think

Please share your thoughts on this book with others by leaving a review on the site that you bought it from. If you purchased the book from Amazon, please leave us an honest review on this book's Amazon page. This is vital so that other potential readers can see and use your unbiased opinion to make purchasing decisions, we can understand what our customers think about our products, and our authors can see your feedback on the title that they have worked with Packt to create. It will only take a few minutes of your time, but is valuable to other potential customers, our authors, and Packt. Thank you!

Index

www.ingramcontent.com/pod-product-compliance
Lightning Source LLC
Chambersburg PA
CBHW080532060326
40690CB00022B/5099

9 781789 807219